MEDITERRANEAN DIET

COOKBOOK FOR BEGINNERS:

2000+ Days of Easy and Healthy Recipes.
Complete 30-Day Meal Plan to Refresh Your
Lifestyle and Everyday Cooking (Full Color Edition)

Linette Johnston

MEDITERRANEAN DIET COOKBOOK FOR BEGINNERS:

2000+ Days of Easy and Healthy Recipes.
Complete 30-Day Meal Plan to Refresh Your Lifestyle and Everyday Cooking (Full Color Edition)

Disclaimer

The information provided in this cookbook, "Mediterranean Diet Cookbook for Beginners," is intended for educational purposes only. It is not intended as a substitute for professional medical advice, diagnosis, or treatment. Always seek the advice of your physician or other qualified health provider with any questions you may have regarding a medical condition. Never disregard professional medical advice or delay in seeking it because of something you have read in this book.

The author and publisher of this book are not responsible for any adverse effects or consequences resulting from the use of any recipes, suggestions, or procedures described in this book. The dietary and nutritional information provided in this book are based on the author's research, knowledge, and personal experience with the Mediterranean diet. Individual results may vary.

The author and publisher make no representations or warranties of any kind with respect to the accuracy, applicability, fitness, or completeness of the contents of this book. The information contained in this book is strictly for educational purposes. If you wish to apply ideas contained in this book, you take full responsibility for your actions.

TABLE OF CONTENTS

INTRODUCTION

Welcome to "The Mediterranean Diet Cookbook for Beginners," your passport to the vibrant and nourishing world of Mediterranean cooking. This isn't just a cookbook; it's a journey into a lifestyle filled with color, flavor, and the joy of cooking.

Imagine the aroma of fresh basil, the sizzle of olive oil, and the rich taste of sun-kissed tomatoes as you bring to life recipes that are as simple as they are delicious. The Mediterranean diet isn't just a way of eating—it's a celebration of each meal as a moment to savor and enjoy. With every recipe, you'll find a fusion of flavors inspired by the shores of Greece, Italy, Spain, Morocco, and beyond.

Inside these pages, you'll uncover the secrets to a healthier, more vibrant life, inspired by the timeless traditions of the Mediterranean. From the tangy zest of a Greek salad to the comforting warmth of a hearty Italian minestrone, this book is packed with recipes that are not only good for your body but also a joy for your taste buds.

Whether you're a culinary novice or a seasoned chef, this cookbook will guide you step-by-step through easy, wholesome recipes that highlight fresh ingredients, bold flavors, and heart-healthy cooking techniques. You'll learn how to create dishes that are as delightful to prepare as they are to share with friends and family.

So, put on your apron, grab that bottle of extra virgin olive oil, and get ready to embark on a culinary adventure where every bite is a step closer to the Mediterranean. Experience the warmth, vitality, and love of Mediterranean cuisine—where each meal is not just food, but a celebration of health, happiness, and togetherness.

Dive into the Mediterranean diet today and discover how easy and delicious healthy eating can be. Let your kitchen be filled with the joy, aromas, and flavors that make the Mediterranean diet a cherished tradition for generations. Bon appétit!

CHAPTER 1. LIFESTYLE ADVICE

The "Mediterranean Diet Cookbook for Beginners" offers an easy-to-follow and delightful approach to adopting healthier eating habits.

This comprehensive guide is designed to maximize your success and enjoyment while adhering to the principles of the Mediterranean diet. We will cover effective meal planning, smart grocery shopping, cooking techniques, tips for dining out, and strategies for overcoming common challenges and temptations.

MEAL PLANNING

Strategies for Creating a Weekly Menu

1. **Balance Nutrient Intake:** Make sure each meal includes a diverse range of nutrients. Aim for a healthy mix of proteins, healthy fats, and carbohydrates. Include a variety of vegetables, fruits, whole grains, legumes, nuts, and seeds to meet your nutritional needs.

2. **Diverse Food Selections:** Rotate different types of proteins (like fish, poultry, or legumes) and vegetables to keep your meals exciting and satisfying. This diversity ensures you get a broad spectrum of vitamins, minerals, and other essential nutrients.

3. **Prepare Ingredients in Advance:** Save time and reduce stress during the week by prepping ingredients in advance—such as chopping vegetables, cooking grains, or marinating proteins. This allows for quicker and easier meal preparation.

4. **Use a Meal Template:** Develop a basic template for your weekly meals. For example, designate Mondays for fish dishes, Tuesdays for vegetarian meals, Wednesdays for poultry, and so on. This approach simplifies meal planning and ensures a variety of nutrients.

GROCERY SHOPPING

Smart Shopping Tips for Success

1. **Read Food Labels Carefully:** Opt for products with minimal ingredients and avoid processed foods. Look out for added sugars, sodium, and unhealthy fats that could undermine your dietary goals.

2. **Choose Fresh, Whole Foods:** Focus on purchasing fresh, whole foods as much as possible. Opt for organic products when available, and prioritize seasonal produce, which tends to be more nutritious and flavorful.

3. **Money-Saving Strategies:** Buy in bulk to save money on staples like nuts, seeds, grains, and legumes. Purchasing seasonal fruits and vegetables can also be cost-effective. Consider joining a local CSA (Community Supported Agriculture) to receive fresh, locally-grown produce.

Essential Items for Your Shopping List

• Fruits and Vegetables: Tomatoes, cucumbers, leafy greens, berries, apples, citrus fruits, peppers, and zucchini.
• Proteins: Fatty fish like salmon, chicken, beans, lentils, chickpeas, and tofu.
• Healthy Fats: Extra virgin olive oil, avocados, nuts (like almonds and walnuts), and seeds (such as chia and flaxseeds).
• Whole Grains: Brown rice, quinoa, whole wheat pasta, barley, and oats.
• Dairy Products: Greek yogurt, feta cheese, ricotta, and other minimally processed cheeses.

COOKING METHODS

Enhancing Flavor While Preserving Nutrition

1. **Grilling and Roasting:** These cooking techniques bring out natural flavors without the need for extra fats. Grilling or roasting vegetables, fish, and lean meats can result in delicious, healthful dishes that retain their nutrients.

2. **Sautéing and Stir-Frying:** Use olive oil for sautéing or stir-frying vegetables and proteins.

These quick methods help preserve the food's nutritional content and natural flavors, making meals both healthy and tasty.

3. **Steaming and Poaching:** Gentle cooking methods like steaming and poaching are excellent for maintaining the texture, color, and nutrients of vegetables, fish, and other delicate ingredients.

4. **Flavor with Herbs and Spices:** Enhance the flavor of your dishes by incorporating fresh herbs like basil, oregano, and rosemary, and spices such as cumin, paprika, and turmeric. These ingredients add depth without extra calories or sodium.

DINING OUT

Sticking to the Diet While Eating Out

1. **Research Menus Ahead of Time:** Before going to a restaurant, look up the menu online and select places that offer Mediterranean-friendly options. This will help you make smarter choices when dining out.

2. **Communicate Your Dietary Preferences:** Don't hesitate to ask your server about how dishes are prepared. Request modifications to suit your dietary needs, such as grilling instead of frying or substituting a side of vegetables.

3. **Make Informed Choices:** Opt for dishes that are grilled, baked, or roasted, and choose salads with olive oil-based dressings. Avoid heavily processed, fried, or overly sauced foods to stay on track with your diet.

4. **Practice Portion Control:** The Mediterranean diet emphasizes moderate portion sizes. Consider sharing dishes with others or asking for a half portion to avoid overeating.

OVERCOMING CHALLENGES

Handling Social Situations and Cravings

1. **Bring a Healthy Dish to Share:** When attending gatherings, potlucks, or parties, bring a dish that aligns with the Mediterranean diet. This way, you ensure there's a healthy option available for you and others.

2. **Keep Healthy Snacks on Hand:** Combat cravings by having nutritious snacks readily available, such as nuts, fruits, or homemade hummus. This prevents reaching for unhealthy options when hunger strikes.

3. **Practice Mindful Eating:** Focus on savoring your food, eating slowly, and being mindful of your hunger and fullness cues. This practice helps prevent overeating and promotes a more satisfying dining experience.

Dealing with Setbacks

1. **Stay Positive and Keep Going:** Don't let occasional slip-ups derail your progress. Acknowledge them as temporary and refocus on your goals with your next meal or day.

2. **Plan Ahead to Avoid Temptations:** Identify potential challenges, such as upcoming social events or travel, and develop strategies to handle them. Having a plan in place will help you stay committed to your goals.

3. **Build a Support Network:** Engage with a community of like-minded individuals or find a diet buddy. Mutual support and motivation can help you stay accountable and inspired on your journey.

CONCLUSION

Adopting the Mediterranean Diet as a beginner can be a deeply rewarding path toward better health and well-being. By implementing these practical tips for meal planning, grocery shopping, cooking, and dining out, you can increase your chances of success and truly enjoy the rich flavors and numerous health benefits of this time-honored eating style. Remember, the keys to success are consistency, variety, and savoring the delicious and nutritious foods that the Mediterranean diet offers. Enjoy your culinary adventure and bon appétit!

CHAPTER 2. BREAKFAST

Mediterranean Shakshuka

Yield: 4 servings
Prep Time: 10 minutes | **Cook Time:** 20 minutes

INGREDIENTS:

- 2 tbsp olive oil (30 ml)
- 1 onion, diced (120g)
- 1 red bell pepper, chopped (150g)
- 3 garlic cloves, minced (9g)
- 1 tsp ground cumin (5g)
- 1 tsp paprika (5g)
- 1/4 tsp chili flakes (optional) (1g)
- 1 can crushed tomatoes (14 oz) (400g)
- Salt and pepper, to taste
- 4 large eggs
- 1/4 cup crumbled feta cheese, optional (40g)
- Fresh parsley, chopped, for garnish

INSTRUCTIONS:

1. Sauté Vegetables: Heat olive oil in a skillet over medium heat. Sauté onion, bell pepper, and garlic until softened.
2. Add Spices: Stir in cumin, paprika, and chili flakes; cook for 1 minute.
3. Cook Sauce: Pour in tomatoes, season with salt and pepper, simmer for 10 minutes.
4. Poach Eggs: Make 4 wells in the sauce, crack an egg into each. Cover skillet and cook until eggs are set to your liking.
5. Finish: Sprinkle with feta and parsley.

NUTRITIONAL INFO (PER SERVING): Calories: 180 | Fat: 11g | Carbs: 15g | Protein: 9g | Fiber: 4g | Sodium: 300mg

Olive Oil and Lemon Pancakes

Yield: 4 servings
Prep Time: 10 minutes | **Cook Time:** 15 minutes

INGREDIENTS:

- 1 cup whole wheat flour (120g)
- 1 tbsp sugar (15g)
- 1 tsp baking powder (5g)
- 1/4 tsp salt (1g)
- 3/4 cup milk (180 ml)
- 2 tbsp olive oil (30 ml)
- 1 large egg
- Zest of 1 lemon
- 1 tbsp lemon juice (15 ml)
- Honey, for drizzling (optional)

INSTRUCTIONS:

1. Mix Dry Ingredients: In a bowl, combine flour, sugar, baking powder, and salt.
2. Prepare Wet Mixture: In another bowl, whisk milk, olive oil, egg, lemon zest, and juice.
3. Combine: Pour wet mixture into dry ingredients, stir until just combined.
4. Cook Pancakes: Heat a skillet over medium heat. Pour batter in small rounds; cook until bubbles form, then flip and cook until golden.

NUTRITIONAL INFO (PER SERVING): Calories: 210 | Fat: 10g | Carbs: 25g | Protein: 6g | Fiber: 2 Sodium: 150mg

Feta and Spinach Omelet

Yield: 1 servings
Prep Time: 5 minutes | **Cook Time:** 5 minutes

INGREDIENTS:

- 2 large eggs
- 1/4 cup fresh spinach, chopped (10g)
- 2 tbsp feta cheese, crumbled (15g)
- 1 tbsp olive oil (15 ml)
- Salt and pepper, to taste
- Fresh dill, chopped (optional)

INSTRUCTIONS:

1. Whisk Eggs: In a bowl, beat the eggs with a pinch of salt and pepper until well mixed.
2. Cook Spinach: Heat olive oil in a skillet over medium heat. Add chopped spinach and sauté for 1-2 minutes until wilted.
3. Make Omelet: Pour the beaten eggs over the spinach in the skillet. Let cook for 2-3 minutes until the edges start to set. Sprinkle feta cheese over the top, then fold the omelet in half and cook for an additional minute until the eggs are fully cooked.
4.Serve: Transfer to a plate and garnish with fresh dill if desired. Serve hot.

NUTRITIONAL INFO (PER SERVING): Calories: 250 | Protein: 14g | Carbohydrates: 2g | Fat: 20g | Fiber: 1g | Sodium: 300mg

Breakfast Couscous with Dried Fruits

Yield: 2 servings
Prep Time: 5 minutes | **Cook Time:** 5 minutes

INGREDIENTS:

- 1 cup couscous (180g)
- 1 cup water (240 ml)
- 1/4 cup dried apricots, chopped (40g)
- 1/4 cup raisins (40g)
- 1/4 cup dried cranberries (40g)
- 1 tbsp honey (15 ml)
- 2 tbsp almonds, chopped (20g)
- Fresh mint, for garnish (optional)

INSTRUCTIONS:

1. Boil Water: Bring water to a boil and pour it over the couscous in a heatproof bowl. Cover tightly with a lid or plate and let it sit for 5 minutes to allow the couscous to absorb the water fully.
2. Add Fruits: Once the couscous is fluffy, stir with a fork to separate the grains, then mix in the dried apricots, raisins, and cranberries, ensuring they are evenly distributed.
3. Serve: Drizzle the mixture with honey for sweetness, then top with chopped almonds for crunch. Garnish with fresh mint leaves if desired, and serve immediately while warm

NUTRITIONAL INFO (PER SERVING): Calories: 300 | Protein: 6g | Carbohydrates: 60g | Fat: 5g | Fiber: 5g | Sodium: 10mg

Overnight Oats with Almonds and Dates

Yield: 2 servings
Prep Time: 5 minutes | **Cook Time:** None

INGREDIENTS:

- 1 cup rolled oats (90g)
- 1 cup almond milk (240 ml)
- 1/4 cup dates, chopped (40g)
- 2 tbsp almonds, sliced (15g)
- 1 tbsp honey (15 ml)
- 1/2 tsp cinnamon (optional)

INSTRUCTIONS:

1. Mix Ingredients: In a jar or a bowl, combine the rolled oats, almond milk, chopped dates, and half of the sliced almonds.
2. Stir well to ensure all the oats are coated with milk and evenly mixed with the dates and almonds.
3. Refrigerate: Cover the jar or bowl with a lid or plastic wrap and place it in the refrigerator.
4. Let it sit overnight (or at least 6 hours) to allow the oats to absorb the liquid and soften.
5. Serve: In the morning, give the oats a good stir and divide them into serving bowls. Top with the remaining sliced almonds, drizzle with honey for sweetness, and sprinkle with cinnamon if desired. Enjoy a ready-to-eat, nutritious breakfast!

NUTRITIONAL INFO (PER SERVING): Calories: 250 | Protein: 6g | Carbohydrates: 45g | Fat: 8g | Fiber: 6g | Sodium: 60mg

Warm Quinoa Porridge with Berries

Yield: 2 servings
Prep Time: 5 minutes | **Cook Time:** 15 minutes

INGREDIENTS:

- 1/2 cup quinoa (90g)
- 1 cup almond milk (240 ml)
- 1/2 cup mixed berries (blueberries, raspberries, strawberries) (75g)
- 1 tbsp honey (15 ml)
- 1 tsp chia seeds (optional)

INSTRUCTIONS:

1. Rinse and Cook Quinoa: Rinse quinoa under cold water.
2. In a saucepan, combine quinoa with almond milk.
3. Bring to a boil, then reduce heat and simmer for about 15 minutes, stirring occasionally, until the quinoa is soft and the milk is mostly absorbed.
4. Adjust Consistency: If needed, add a bit more almond milk to achieve your preferred porridge consistency. Stir well and let it warm for another minute.
5. Serve: Divide the quinoa porridge into bowls, top with mixed berries, drizzle with honey, and sprinkle with chia seeds, if using. Serve warm.

NUTRITIONAL INFO (PER SERVING): Calories: 230 | Protein: 7g | Carbohydrates: 38g | Fat: 6g | Fiber: 5g | Sodium: 40mg

Mediterranean Frittata

Yield: 4 servings
Prep Time: 10 minutes | **Cook Time:** 20 minutes

INGREDIENTS:

- 6 large eggs (300g)
- 1/2 cup bell peppers, diced (75g)
- 1/2 cup spinach, chopped (15g)
- 1/4 cup cherry tomatoes, halved (40g)
- 1/4 cup feta cheese, crumbled (30g)
- 1 tbsp olive oil (15 ml)
- Salt and pepper, to taste
- Fresh herbs (parsley, dill) for garnish

INSTRUCTIONS:

1. Preheat Oven: Set to 375°F (190°C).
2. Sauté Vegetables: In a skillet, heat olive oil, add bell peppers and spinach; cook until soft.
3. Add Eggs: Whisk eggs with salt and pepper, pour over vegetables. Top with tomatoes and feta.
4. Bake: Transfer skillet to oven, bake for 15 minutes until eggs are set.
5. Garnish and Serve: Sprinkle with fresh herbs.

NUTRITIONAL INFO (PER SERVING): Calories: 180 | Protein: 12g | Carbohydrates: 4g | Fat: 13g | Fiber: 1g | Sodium: 220mg

Greek Yogurt Parfait with Fresh Fruit

Yield: 2 servings
Prep Time: 5 minutes | **Cook Time:** None

INGREDIENTS:

- 1 cup Greek yogurt (240g)
- 1/2 cup mixed berries (strawberries, blueberries, raspberries) (75g)
- 1/4 cup granola (30g)
- 1 tbsp honey (15 ml)
- Fresh mint leaves for garnish (optional)

INSTRUCTIONS:

1. Layer Parfait: In two serving jars or glasses, begin by spooning a layer of Greek yogurt at the bottom.
2. Next, add a layer of mixed berries, followed by a sprinkle of granola.
3. Repeat the layers until all ingredients are used, ending with a layer of granola on top.
4. Finish: Drizzle each parfait with honey to add natural sweetness. Garnish with a few fresh mint leaves for a refreshing touch, if desired.
5. Serve immediately or refrigerate for up to an hour for a cool, refreshing treat.

NUTRITIONAL INFO (PER SERVING): Calories: 180 | Protein: 10g | Carbohydrates: 20g | Fat: 5g | Fiber: 3g | Sodium: 50mg

Hummus and Veggie Breakfast Wrap

Yield: 2 servings
Prep Time: 5 minutes | **Cook Time:** None

INGREDIENTS:

- 2 whole wheat tortillas (50g each)
- 1/2 cup hummus (120g)
- 1/2 cucumber, sliced (60g)
- 1/2 bell pepper, sliced (50g)
- 1/2 cup cherry tomatoes, halved (75g)
- 1/2 cup fresh spinach leaves (15g)
- Fresh parsley for garnish (optional)

INSTRUCTIONS:

1. Assemble Wraps: Lay the whole wheat tortillas flat on a clean surface.
2. Evenly spread a layer of hummus over each tortilla, covering most of the surface.
3. Arrange the sliced cucumber, bell pepper, cherry tomatoes, and fresh spinach leaves evenly on top of the hummus.
4. Wrap and Serve: Carefully roll up each tortilla tightly, making sure the filling is secure inside. Slice the wraps in half if desired. Garnish with fresh parsley for added flavor and color.
5. Serve immediately for a fresh and healthy breakfast or snack option.

NUTRITIONAL INFO (PER SERVING): Calories: 250 | Protein: 8g | Carbohydrates: 30g | Fat: 10g | Fiber: 7g | Sodium: 300mg

Spinach and Ricotta Stuffed Peppers

Yield: 4 servings
Prep Time: 10 minutes | **Cook Time:** 30 minutes

INGREDIENTS:

- 4 bell peppers, halved and seeded (400g)
- 1 cup ricotta cheese (250g)
- 2 cups fresh spinach, sautéed (60g)
- 1/4 cup Parmesan cheese, grated (25g)
- Salt and pepper, to taste
- Fresh basil, chopped (optional)

INSTRUCTIONS:

1. Preheat Oven: Preheat your oven to 375°F (190°C) to get it ready for baking.
2. Mix Filling: In a medium-sized bowl, combine the ricotta cheese, sautéed spinach, grated Parmesan, salt, and pepper. Mix well.
3. Stuff Peppers: Arrange the halved and seeded bell peppers in a baking dish. Fill each pepper half generously with the ricotta and spinach mixture, pressing it down slightly to ensure it's well-packed.
4. Bake: Place the baking dish in the preheated oven and bake for 30 minutes or until the peppers are tender and the filling is lightly golden on top.
5. For an extra touch, garnish with freshly chopped basil before serving.

NUTRITIONAL INFO (PER SERVING): Calories: 200 | Protein: 10g | Carbohydrates: 10g | Fat: 12g | Fiber: 3g | Sodium: 180mg

Fresh Fruit Salad with Citrus Dressing

Yield: 4 servings
Prep Time: 10 minutes | **Cook Time:** None

INGREDIENTS:

- 1 cup strawberries, sliced (150g)
- 1 cup blueberries (150g)
- 1 kiwi, peeled and sliced (75g)
- 1 orange, segmented (100g)
- 2 tbsp orange juice (30ml)
- 1 tbsp lemon juice (15ml)
- 1 tsp honey (7g)
- Fresh mint leaves for garnish (optional)

INSTRUCTIONS:

1. Combine Fruits: In a large mixing bowl, gently combine the sliced strawberries, blueberries, kiwi slices, and orange segments. Toss the fruits together to ensure they are evenly mixed, creating a colorful and vibrant base for the salad.
2. Make Dressing: In a small bowl, whisk together the orange juice, lemon juice, and honey until the honey is fully dissolved and the dressing is smooth.
3. Drizzle and Garnish: Pour the citrus dressing over the fruit mixture and gently toss to coat the fruits evenly. Garnish with fresh mint leaves for an added hint of freshness and a pop of green color.
4. Serve immediately for the best taste and texture.

NUTRITIONAL INFO (PER SERVING): Calories: 80 | Protein: 1g | Carbohydrates: 20g | Fat: 0g | Fiber: 4g | Sodium: 0mg

Millet Porridge with Almond Milk

Yield: 2 servings
Prep Time: 5 minutes | **Cook Time:** 20 minutes

INGREDIENTS:

- 1/2 cup millet (90g)
- 1 1/2 cups almond milk (360ml)
- 1 tbsp honey (21g)
- Fresh blueberries for topping
- Sliced almonds for topping
- Fresh mint (optional)

INSTRUCTIONS:

1. Cook Millet: In a medium-sized saucepan, combine the millet and almond milk.
2. Bring the mixture to a gentle boil over medium heat. Once it starts to boil, reduce the heat to low and let it simmer for about 20 minutes, stirring occasionally, until the millet is tender and the porridge reaches a creamy consistency. If it becomes too thick, add a bit more almond milk.
3. Serve: Spoon the creamy millet porridge into bowls. Drizzle each serving with honey for a touch of sweetness, then top with fresh blueberries and sliced almonds for added texture and flavor. Garnish with fresh mint leaves if desired.
4. Enjoy this warm and comforting breakfast that is both healthy and delicious.

NUTRITIONAL INFO (PER SERVING): Calories: 220 | Protein: 6g | Carbohydrates: 40g | Fats: 5g | Fiber: 4g | Sodium: 80mg

Breakfast Couscous Salad

Yield: 2 servings
Prep Time: 5 minutes | **Cook Time:** 5 minutes

INGREDIENTS:

- 1/2 cup couscous (90g)
- 1/2 cup boiling water (120ml)
- 1/2 cup cucumber, diced (75g)
- 1/2 cup cherry tomatoes, halved (75g)
- 2 tbsp feta cheese, crumbled (30g)
- 1 tbsp olive oil (15ml)
- 1 tbsp lemon juice (15ml)
- Fresh parsley, chopped (for garnish)

INSTRUCTIONS:

1. Prepare Couscous: Place the couscous in a bowl and pour the boiling water over it.
2. Cover the bowl with a lid or a plate and let it sit for 5 minutes. Once done, fluff the couscous with a fork.
3. Mix Salad: Add the diced cucumber, halved cherry tomatoes, crumbled feta cheese, olive oil, lemon juice, and chopped fresh parsley to the couscous. Gently toss everything together until all the ingredients are well mixed and evenly coated with the dressing.
4. Serve immediately or chill in the fridge for a refreshing, quick, and healthy breakfast option.

NUTRITIONAL INFO (PER SERVING): Calories: 180 | Protein: 6g | Carbohydrates: 28g | Fats: 6g | Fiber: 3g | Sodium: 150mg

Baked Oatmeal with Apples and Cinnamon

Yield: 4 servings
Prep Time: 10 minutes | **Cook Time:** 30 minutes

INGREDIENTS:

- 1 cup rolled oats (90g)
- 1 1/2 cups almond milk (360ml)
- 1 apple, diced (150g)
- 1/4 cup honey (60ml)
- 1 tsp cinnamon (2g)
- 1/2 tsp baking powder (2g)
- 1/4 tsp salt (1.5g)

INSTRUCTIONS:

1. Preheat Oven: Preheat your oven to 350°F (175°C).
2. Grease a baking dish with a bit of oil or cooking spray to prevent sticking.
3. Mix Ingredients: In a large mixing bowl, combine the rolled oats, almond milk, diced apple, honey, cinnamon, baking powder, and salt. Stir well to ensure that all the ingredients are evenly distributed and the oats are coated with the liquid.
4. Bake: Pour the mixture into the prepared baking dish, spreading it out evenly. Place the dish in the preheated oven and bake for about 30 minutes or until the oatmeal is set and the top is lightly golden.
5. Let it cool for a few minutes before serving.

NUTRITIONAL INFO (PER SERVING): Calories: 200 | Protein: 5g | Carbohydrates: 38g | Fats: 4g | Fiber: 5g | Sodium: 100mg

Mediterranean Smoothie Bowl

Yield: 1 servings
Prep Time: 5 minutes | **Cook Time:** None

INGREDIENTS:

- 1/2 cup Greek yogurt (120g)
- 1/2 cup frozen berries (75g)
- 1/2 banana (50g)
- 1/4 cup almond milk (60ml)
- 2 tbsp granola (30g)
- 1 tsp chia seeds (5g)
- Fresh mint (optional)

INSTRUCTIONS:

1. Blend Base: In a blender, combine the Greek yogurt, frozen berries, banana, and almond milk.
2. Blend until smooth and creamy, making sure there are no chunks remaining. If the mixture is too thick, add a little more almond milk to reach your desired consistency.
3. Assemble Bowl: Pour the smoothie into a bowl and smooth the top with a spoon.
4. Top with granola for crunch, chia seeds for added nutrition, and a few fresh mint leaves for a refreshing touch.

NUTRITIONAL INFO (PER SERVING): Calories: 220 | Protein: 8g | Carbohydrates: 35g | Fats: 6g | Fiber: 6g | Sodium: 70mg

Honey and Almond Granola

Yield: 4 servings
Prep Time: 5 minutes | **Cook Time:** 20 minutes

INGREDIENTS:

- 2 cups rolled oats (180g)
- 1/2 cup almonds, sliced (75g)
- 2 tbsp honey (30g)
- 2 tbsp olive oil (30ml)
- 1/4 cup seeds (pumpkin, sunflower) (40g)
- 1/2 tsp cinnamon (optional) (1g)

INSTRUCTIONS:

1. Preheat Oven: Preheat your oven to 325°F (160°C). Line a baking sheet with parchment paper to prevent sticking.
2. Mix Ingredients: In a large bowl, combine the rolled oats, sliced almonds, seeds, honey, olive oil, and cinnamon if using. Mix well to ensure all the oats and nuts are coated with honey and oil, which helps them crisp up nicely while baking.
3. Bake: Spread the mixture evenly on the prepared baking sheet. Bake for 20 minutes, stirring halfway through to ensure even baking. The granola should be golden and slightly crisp. Let it cool completely before storing it in an airtight container. This homemade granola is perfect for topping yogurt, smoothie bowls, or enjoying as a snack.

NUTRITIONAL INFO (PER SERVING): Calories: 250 | Protein: 6g | Carbohydrates: 32g | Fats: 12g | Fiber: 4g | Sodium: 5mg

CHAPTER 3. SALADS

Greek Salad with Feta and Olives

Yield: 4 servings
Prep Time: 10 minutes | **Cook Time:** None

INGREDIENTS:

- 2 cups tomatoes, chopped (300g)
- 1 cucumber, sliced (200g)
- 1/2 red onion, thinly sliced (75g)
- 1/2 cup Kalamata olives (75g)
- 1/2 cup feta cheese, crumbled (75g)
- 2 tbsp olive oil (30ml)
- 1 tbsp red wine vinegar (15ml)
- Fresh oregano, chopped (to taste)
- Salt and pepper, to taste

INSTRUCTIONS:

1. Prepare Salad: In a large bowl, mix the chopped tomatoes, sliced cucumber, thinly sliced red onion, Kalamata olives, and crumbled feta cheese. Ensure all ingredients are well distributed.

2. Dress Salad: Drizzle the salad with olive oil and red wine vinegar. Add salt, pepper, and chopped fresh oregano to taste. Toss gently to combine, making sure the dressing coats all the ingredients evenly.

NUTRITIONAL INFO (PER SERVING): Calories: 150 | Protein: 4g | Carbohydrates: 8g | Fats: 12g | Fiber: 2g | Sodium: 350mg

Quinoa Tabbouleh with Fresh Herbs

Yield: 4 servings
Prep Time: 10 minutes | **Cook Time:** 15 minutes

INGREDIENTS:

- 1 cup quinoa, cooked (185g)
- 1 cup parsley, chopped (60g)
- 1/2 cup mint, chopped (30g)
- 1 cup tomatoes, diced (150g)
- 1/2 cucumber, diced (100g)
- 1/4 cup red onion, chopped (40g)
- 2 tbsp olive oil (30ml)
- 2 tbsp lemon juice (30ml)
- Salt and pepper, to taste

INSTRUCTIONS:

1. Combine Ingredients: In a large bowl, mix the cooked quinoa, chopped parsley, chopped mint, diced tomatoes, diced cucumber, and chopped red onion. Make sure all the ingredients are well combined.

2. Dress Salad: Add olive oil, lemon juice, salt, and pepper to the mixture. Toss everything well to ensure the dressing is evenly distributed throughout the salad.

NUTRITIONAL INFO (PER SERVING): Calories: 180 | Protein: 5g | Carbohydrates: 20g | Fats: 8g | Fiber: 4g | Sodium: 50mg

Mediterranean Chickpea Salad

Yield: 4 servings
Prep Time: 10 minutes | **Cook Time:** None

INGREDIENTS:

- 1 can (15 oz) chickpeas, drained and rinsed (425g)
- 1 cup tomatoes, diced (150g)
- 1/2 cucumber, diced (100g)
- 1/4 cup red onion, chopped (40g)
- 1/4 cup Kalamata olives, sliced (30g)
- 2 tbsp parsley, chopped (8g)
- 2 tbsp olive oil (30ml)
- 1 tbsp lemon juice (15ml)
- Salt and pepper, to taste

INSTRUCTIONS:

1. Mix Salad: In a bowl, combine the chickpeas, diced tomatoes, diced cucumber, chopped red onion, sliced Kalamata olives, and chopped parsley. Mix well to distribute the ingredients evenly.
2. Dress Salad: Add olive oil, lemon juice, salt, and pepper. Toss to coat all the ingredients with the dressing.

NUTRITIONAL INFO (PER SERVING): Calories: 150 | Protein: 5g | Carbohydrates: 18g | Fats: 7g | Fiber: 5g | Sodium: 300mg

Tomato and Cucumber Salad with Red Onion

Yield: 4 servings
Prep Time: 10 minutes | **Cook Time:** None

INGREDIENTS:

- 2 cups tomatoes, diced (300g)
- 1 cucumber, sliced (200g)
- 1/4 cup red onion, thinly sliced (40g)
- 2 tbsp olive oil (30ml)
- 1 tbsp lemon juice (15ml)
- Fresh parsley, chopped
- Salt and pepper, to taste

INSTRUCTIONS:

1. Combine Ingredients: In a large bowl, mix together the diced tomatoes, sliced cucumber, and thinly sliced red onion. Toss gently to ensure all vegetables are well combined.
2. Dress Salad: Drizzle the olive oil and lemon juice over the mixture. Season generously with salt and pepper, then toss everything thoroughly so that the dressing evenly coats the vegetables.
3. Let Rest: Allow the salad to sit for 5-10 minutes to let the flavors blend, or refrigerate briefly before serving for a more refreshing taste.
4. Serve: Garnish with freshly chopped parsley before serving for added freshness.

NUTRITIONAL INFO (PER SERVING): Calories: 80 | Protein: 1g | Carbohydrates: 6g | Fats: 6g | Fiber: 2g | Sodium: 100mg

Lentil Salad with Fresh Mint and Feta

Yield: 4 servings
Prep Time: 10 minutes | **Cook Time:** 20 minutes

INGREDIENTS:

- 1 cup lentils, cooked (200g)
- 1 cup tomatoes, diced (150g)
- 1/2 cucumber, diced (100g)
- 1/4 cup feta cheese, crumbled (40g)
- 2 tbsp fresh mint, chopped (8g)
- 2 tbsp olive oil (30ml)
- 1 tbsp lemon juice (15ml)
- Salt and pepper, to taste

INSTRUCTIONS:

1. Mix Salad: In a large mixing bowl, combine the cooked lentils, diced tomatoes, diced cucumber, crumbled feta cheese, and chopped fresh mint. Stir gently, taking care not to mash the lentils.
2. Dress Salad: Drizzle the olive oil and lemon juice over the salad. Season with salt and pepper to taste. Toss carefully to coat the ingredients with the dressing, ensuring an even distribution.
3. Let Flavors Meld: Allow the salad to sit for 5-10 minutes to let the flavors meld together, enhancing the freshness of the mint and the sharpness of the feta.
4. Serve: Serve the salad chilled or at room temperature.

NUTRITIONAL INFO (PER SERVING): Calories: 150 | Protein: 6g | Carbohydrates: 18g | Fats: 7g | Fiber: 5g | Sodium: 180mg.

Grilled Chicken Caesar Salad

Yield: 2 servings
Prep Time: 10 minutes | **Cook Time:** 15 minutes

INGREDIENTS:

- 2 chicken breasts, grilled and sliced (300g)
- 4 cups romaine lettuce, chopped (150g)
- 1/4 cup Parmesan cheese, shaved (25g)
- 1/2 cup croutons (30g)
- 2 tbsp Caesar dressing (30ml)
- Lemon wedges, for serving
- Salt and pepper, to taste

INSTRUCTIONS:

1. Grill Chicken: Season the chicken breasts with salt and pepper. Grill them until fully cooked, then slice them into thin strips.
2. Assemble Salad: In a large bowl, mix the chopped romaine lettuce, grilled chicken slices, shaved Parmesan cheese, and croutons. Add Caesar dressing and toss everything together until well coated.
3. Serve: Serve the salad with lemon wedges and a sprinkle of black pepper on top.

NUTRITIONAL INFO (PER SERVING): Calories: 320 | Protein: 30g | Carbohydrates: 12g | Fats: 18g | Fiber: 3g | Sodium: 420mg.

Roasted Vegetable and Arugula Salad

Yield: 4 servings
Prep Time: 10 minutes | **Cook Time:** 20

INGREDIENTS:

- 1 zucchini, sliced
- 1 bell pepper, chopped
- 1 cup cherry tomatoes
- 1/2 red onion, sliced
- 2 cups arugula
- 1/4 cup feta cheese, crumbled (40g)
- 2 tbsp pine nuts (30g)
- 2 tbsp olive oil (30ml)
- 1 tbsp balsamic vinegar (15ml)
- Salt and pepper, to taste

INSTRUCTIONS:

1. Roast Vegetables: Preheat the oven to 400°F (200°C). Toss the sliced zucchini, chopped bell pepper, cherry tomatoes, and sliced red onion with olive oil, salt, and pepper. Spread them on a baking sheet and roast for about 20 minutes, or until tender and slightly caramelized.

2. Assemble Salad: In a large bowl, combine the roasted vegetables with fresh arugula, crumbled feta cheese, and pine nuts. Drizzle with balsamic vinegar and toss everything together.

NUTRITIONAL INFO (PER SERVING): Calories: 180 | Protein: 5g | Carbohydrates: 12g | Fats: 14g | Fiber: 3g | Sodium: 150mg

Spinach Salad with Oranges and Almonds

Yield: 4 servings
Prep Time: 10 minutes | **Cook Time:** None

INGREDIENTS:

- 4 cups baby spinach
- 2 oranges, segmented
- 1/4 cup sliced almonds (30g)
- 1/4 cup feta cheese, crumbled (40g)
- 2 tbsp olive oil (30ml)
- 1 tbsp orange juice (15ml)
- Salt and pepper, to taste

INSTRUCTIONS:

1. Mix Salad: In a large bowl, combine the baby spinach, orange segments, sliced almonds, and crumbled feta cheese. Toss gently, ensuring the oranges and almonds are spread out for a balanced bite.

2. Dress Salad: Drizzle the olive oil and orange juice over the salad. Add a pinch of salt and a few cracks of black pepper. Toss the salad lightly, ensuring all the spinach leaves are coated with the dressing without crushing the orange segments.

3. Let it Rest: Allow the salad to sit for a minute or two to let the flavors meld.

4. Serve: Serve immediately as a fresh and vibrant side dish or light meal.

NUTRITIONAL INFO (PER SERVING): Calories: 130 | Protein: 3g | Carbohydrates: 10g | Fat: 9g | Fiber: 3g | Sodium: 100mg

Mixed Green Salad with Pear and Gorgonzola

Yield: 4 servings
Prep Time: 10 minutes | **Cook Time:** None

INGREDIENTS:

- 4 cups mixed greens (arugula, spinach, romaine)
- 1 ripe pear, thinly sliced
- 75g crumbled gorgonzola cheese
- 1/4 cup walnuts, toasted (30g)
- 2 tbsp olive oil (30ml)
- 1 tbsp balsamic vinegar (15ml)
- 1 tsp honey (optional)
- Salt and pepper, to taste
- Fresh basil or parsley for garnish (optional)

INSTRUCTIONS:

1. Prepare Salad: Combine the mixed greens in a large bowl. Use a variety of textures for balance.
2. Add Toppings: Layer the pear slices, crumbled gorgonzola, and toasted walnuts over the greens for a vibrant, balanced look.
3. Make Dressing: Whisk together olive oil, balsamic vinegar, honey (if using), salt, and pepper until smooth.
4. Toss Salad: Drizzle the dressing over the salad, tossing lightly to ensure even coverage.
5. Garnish: Add a sprinkle of fresh herbs like parsley or basil for a burst of flavor and visual appeal. Serve immediately.

NUTRITIONAL INFO (PER SERVING): Calories: 210 | Protein: 5g | Carbohydrates: 12g | Fats: 17g | Fiber: 3g | Sodium: 220mg

Tuna Salad with White Beans

Yield: 4 servings
Prep Time: 10 minutes | **Cook Time:** None

INGREDIENTS:

- 2 cans tuna, drained (about 280g)
- 1 cup white beans, drained and rinsed (170g)
- 1/2 cup tomatoes, diced (75g)
- 1/4 cup red onion, chopped (40g)
- 2 tbsp olive oil (30ml)
- 1 tbsp lemon juice (15ml)
- Fresh parsley, chopped
- Salt and pepper, to taste

INSTRUCTIONS:

1. Mix Salad: In a large mixing bowl, add the drained tuna and white beans. Break up the tuna slightly with a fork but keep it chunky for texture. Add the diced tomatoes, chopped red onion, and freshly chopped parsley to the bowl. Stir everything gently.
2. Dress Salad: Drizzle the olive oil and lemon juice over the salad mixture. Season with salt and pepper. Toss everything.
3. Serve: Transfer the salad to individual plates or a serving bowl. Garnish with extra parsley if desired and serve immediately, or refrigerate for 10-15 minutes.

NUTRITIONAL INFO (PER SERVING): Calories: 200 | Protein: 18g | Carbohydrates: 12g | Fats: 8g | Fiber: 4g | Sodium: 250mg

Farro Salad with Roasted Red Peppers

Yield: 4 servings
Prep Time: 10 minutes | **Cook Time:** 20 minutes

INGREDIENTS:

- 1 cup farro, cooked (200g)
- 1/2 cup roasted red peppers, sliced (75g)
- 1/2 cup cucumber, diced (100g)
- 1/2 cup cherry tomatoes, halved (75g)
- 1/4 cup feta cheese, crumbled (30g)
- 2 tbsp olive oil (30ml)
- 1 tbsp balsamic vinegar (15ml)
- Fresh parsley, chopped
- Salt and pepper, to taste

INSTRUCTIONS:

1. Cook Farro: If not already cooked, boil the farro in salted water for about 20 minutes, then drain and let cool slightly.
2. Combine Ingredients: In a large bowl, add the cooked farro, roasted red peppers, cucumber, cherry tomatoes, and feta. Sprinkle with chopped parsley and gently toss to combine.
3. Dress Salad: Drizzle with olive oil and balsamic vinegar. Season with salt and pepper, then toss again to evenly coat the ingredients.
4. Serve: Transfer to a serving dish and enjoy.

NUTRITIONAL INFO (PER SERVING): Calories: 220 | Protein: 6g | Carbohydrates: 32g | Fats: 9g | Fiber: 5g | Sodium: 150mg

Beet and Goat Cheese Salad

Yield: 4 servings
Prep Time: 10 minutes | **Cook Time:** 30 minutes

INGREDIENTS:

- 2 large beets, roasted and sliced
- 4 cups mixed greens (arugula, spinach, romaine)
- 1/4 cup goat cheese, crumbled (30g)
- 1/4 cup walnuts, chopped (30g)
- 2 tbsp olive oil (30ml)
- 1 tbsp balsamic vinegar (15ml)
- Fresh basil, chopped
- Salt and pepper, to taste

INSTRUCTIONS:

1. Roast Beets: Preheat the oven to 400°F (200°C). Wrap the beets in foil and roast for 30-40 minutes, until tender. Allow them to cool before peeling and slicing.
2. Assemble Salad: In a large bowl, layer the mixed greens. Add the roasted beet slices, crumbled goat cheese, and chopped walnuts.
3. Dress Salad: Drizzle the olive oil and balsamic vinegar over the salad. Season with salt and pepper.
4. Garnish: Sprinkle fresh basil on top and serve immediately.

NUTRITIONAL INFO (PER SERVING): Calories: 180 | Protein: 5g | Carbohydrates: 15g | Fats: 12g | Fiber: 3g | Sodium: 150mg

Shrimp and Avocado Salad

Yield: 4 servings
Prep Time: 10 minutes | **Cook Time:** 5 minutes

INGREDIENTS:

- 1 lb shrimp, grilled
- 2 avocados, diced
- 1 cup cherry tomatoes, halved
- 4 cups mixed greens
- 2 tbsp olive oil
- 1 tbsp lemon juice
- Fresh cilantro, chopped
- Salt and pepper, to taste

INSTRUCTIONS:

1. Grill the Shrimp: Preheat a grill or stovetop grill pan to medium heat. Lightly coat the shrimp with olive oil, salt, and pepper. Grill the shrimp for 2-3 minutes per side until pink and opaque. Set aside to cool slightly.
2. Prepare Salad: Dice the avocados and halve the cherry tomatoes. In a large bowl, layer the mixed greens, tomatoes, and avocado.
3. Combine Ingredients: Add the grilled shrimp to the bowl.
4. Dress Salad: Drizzle with olive oil and lemon juice. Season with salt and pepper.
5. Toss and Garnish: Gently toss to coat. Garnish with fresh chopped cilantro.

NUTRITIONAL INFO (PER SERVING): Calories: 250 | Protein: 18g | Carbohydrates: 10g | Fats: 18g | Fiber: 6g | Sodium: 220mg

Roasted Beet and Citrus Salad

Yield: 4 servings
Prep Time: 10 minutes | **Cook Time:** 30 minutes

INGREDIENTS:

- 2 beets, roasted and sliced
- 1 orange, segmented
- 1 grapefruit, segmented
- 4 cups mixed greens
- 2 tbsp olive oil
- 1 tbsp lemon juice
- Fresh mint leaves
- Salt and pepper, to taste

INSTRUCTIONS:

1. Roast the Beets: Preheat your oven to 400°F (200°C). Wrap the beets in foil and roast for about 30 minutes or until tender. Allow them to cool slightly before peeling and slicing them.
2. Assemble Salad: In a large bowl, combine the roasted and sliced beets with the segmented orange and grapefruit. Add the mixed greens to the bowl.
3. Dress Salad: Drizzle the olive oil and lemon juice over the salad. Season with salt and pepper.
4. Toss and Garnish: Gently toss everything to combine. Garnish with fresh mint leaves for added freshness.

NUTRITIONAL INFO (PER SERVING): Calories: 120 | Protein: 2g | Carbohydrates: 18g | Fats: 6g | Fiber: 4g | Sodium: 50mg

Cucumber and Dill Salad with Yogurt Dressing

Yield: 4 servings
Prep Time: 10 minutes | **Cook Time:** None

INGREDIENTS:

- 2 cucumbers, sliced
- 1/4 red onion, thinly sliced
- 1/2 cup Greek yogurt
- 1 tbsp fresh dill, chopped
- 1 tbsp lemon juice
- Salt and pepper, to taste

INSTRUCTIONS:

1. Mix Salad: In a medium-sized bowl, combine the sliced cucumbers, thinly sliced red onion, Greek yogurt, chopped dill, and lemon juice. Stir gently until all ingredients are mixed well, ensuring the yogurt coats the cucumbers and onions.
2. Season: Sprinkle with salt and pepper to taste. Toss the salad gently again to ensure even seasoning and a smooth, creamy consistency.
3. Chill: Refrigerate the salad for about 5 minutes to let the flavors meld, enhancing the freshness of the cucumbers and dill.
4. Serve: Serve chilled as a refreshing side dish, perfect for warm days or as an accompaniment to grilled meats.

NUTRITIONAL INFO (PER SERVING): Calories: 70 | Protein: 3g | Carbohydrates: 8g | Fats: 3g | Fiber: 1g | Sodium: 30mg

Grilled Halloumi and Vegetable Salad

Yield: 4 servings
Prep Time: 10 minutes | **Cook Time:** 10 minutes

INGREDIENTS:

- 8 oz halloumi cheese, sliced
- 1 bell pepper, sliced
- 1 zucchini, sliced
- 1 cup cherry tomatoes
- 4 cups mixed greens
- 2 tbsp olive oil
- Fresh herbs (basil, parsley)
- Salt and pepper, to taste

INSTRUCTIONS:

1. Grill Ingredients: Grill the halloumi slices, bell pepper, zucchini, and cherry tomatoes until they are charred and tender.
2. Assemble Salad: Arrange the grilled vegetables and halloumi on a bed of mixed greens. Garnish with fresh herbs like basil and parsley.
3. Dress Salad: Drizzle with olive oil and season with salt and pepper.
4. Serve immediately.

NUTRITIONAL INFO (PER SERVING): Calories: 220 | Protein: 12g | Carbohydrates: 6g | Fats: 16g | Fiber: 2g | Sodium: 400mg

Arugula Salad with Prosciutto and Melon

Yield: 4 servings
Prep Time: 10 minutes | **Cook Time:** None

INGREDIENTS:

- 4 cups arugula
- 4 slices prosciutto, torn
- 1 cup melon, balled or cubed
- 1 tbsp olive oil
- 1 tbsp balsamic glaze
- Black pepper, to taste

INSTRUCTIONS:

1. Prepare Ingredients: Gently rinse and pat dry the arugula. Tear the prosciutto into bite-sized pieces and cut the melon into either balls or cubes for easy serving.
2. Assemble Salad: On a serving plate, arrange a bed of arugula. Evenly scatter the torn prosciutto and melon pieces over the greens.
3. Dress Salad: Drizzle the olive oil and balsamic glaze over the salad. Add a light sprinkle of black pepper to taste.
4. Serve Immediately: Serve the salad right away to enjoy the fresh flavors and crisp textures.

NUTRITIONAL INFO (PER SERVING): Calories: 140 | Protein: 5g | Carbs: 10g | Fats: 9g | Fiber: 2g | Sodium: 300mg

Carrot and Orange Salad with Walnuts

Yield: 4 servings
Prep Time: 10 minutes | **Cook Time:** None

INGREDIENTS:

- 2 cups carrots, thinly sliced
- 2 oranges, segmented
- 1/4 cup walnuts, chopped
- 2 tbsp olive oil
- 1 tbsp lemon juice
- Fresh mint leaves
- Salt and pepper, to taste

INSTRUCTIONS:

1. Prepare Ingredients: Peel and thinly slice the carrots using a sharp knife or mandoline for even slices. Segment the oranges by cutting away the peel and pith, then cutting out the flesh between the membranes.
2. Mix Salad: In a large bowl, combine the thinly sliced carrots, segmented oranges, and chopped walnuts. Make sure the ingredients are evenly mixed.
3. Dress Salad: Drizzle the olive oil and lemon juice over the salad. Season with salt and pepper, then toss gently.
4. Garnish and Serve: Garnish the salad with fresh mint leaves for added flavor and freshness. Serve immediately for the best texture and taste.

NUTRITIONAL INFO (PER SERVING): Calories: 130 | Protein: 2g | Carbs: 12g | Fats: 9g | Fiber: 3g | Sodium: 20mg

Roasted Sweet Potato and Feta Salad

Yield: 4 servings
Prep Time: 10 minutes | **Cook Time:** 25 minutes

INGREDIENTS:

- 2 cups sweet potatoes, cubed
- 1/4 cup feta cheese, crumbled
- 2 cups arugula
- 1/2 cup cherry tomatoes, halved
- 2 tbsp olive oil
- 1 tbsp balsamic vinegar
- Salt and pepper, to taste

INSTRUCTIONS:

1. Roast Sweet Potatoes: Preheat the oven to 400°F (200°C). Toss the cubed sweet potatoes with olive oil, salt, and pepper. Spread them on a baking sheet and roast for about 25 minutes, or until tender and slightly caramelized.

2. Assemble Salad: In a large bowl, mix the arugula, halved cherry tomatoes, roasted sweet potatoes, and crumbled feta. Drizzle with balsamic vinegar and toss to combine.

NUTRITIONAL INFO (PER SERVING): Calories: 160 | Protein: 4g | Carbs: 20g | Fats: 8g | Fiber: 4g | Sodium: 250mg

Grilled Salmon Salad with Lemon Dressing

Yield: 4 servings
Prep Time: 10 minutes | **Cook Time:** 10 minutes

INGREDIENTS:

- 4 salmon fillets
- 4 cups mixed greens
- 1 cup cherry tomatoes, halved
- 1 cucumber, sliced
- 1/4 red onion, thinly sliced
- 3 tbsp olive oil
- 2 tbsp lemon juice
- Fresh dill, chopped
- Salt and pepper, to taste

INSTRUCTIONS:

1. Grill Salmon: Season the salmon fillets with salt and pepper. Grill them for 4-5 minutes on each side, or until fully cooked and flaky.

2. Assemble Salad: On a large serving platter, arrange the mixed greens, halved cherry tomatoes, sliced cucumber, thinly sliced red onion, and grilled salmon.

3. Dress Salad: Drizzle with olive oil and lemon juice. Garnish with fresh dill and serve immediately.

NUTRITIONAL NFO (PER SERVING): Calories: 300 | Protein: 25g | Carbs: 8g | Fats: 18g | Fiber: 2g | Sodium: 150mg

CHAPTER 4. MEAT AND POULTRY

Chicken Souvlaki with Garlic Sauce

Yield: 4 servings
Prep Time: 15 minutes | **Cook Time:** 15 minutes

INGREDIENTS:

- 1 lb chicken breast, cubed
- 2 tbsp olive oil
- 2 tbsp lemon juice
- 2 garlic cloves, minced
- 1 tsp oregano
- Salt and pepper, to taste

Garlic Sauce:
- 1/2 cup Greek yogurt
- 1 garlic clove, minced
- 1 tbsp lemon juice
- Salt to taste

INSTRUCTIONS:

1. **Marinate Chicken:** Mix olive oil, lemon juice, garlic, oregano, salt, and pepper. Marinate chicken for 30 minutes.
2. **Grill Chicken:** Skewer chicken and grill for 10-12 minutes, turning occasionally.
3. **Prepare Sauce:** Mix yogurt, garlic, lemon juice, and salt.
4. **Serve:** Plate chicken with sauce and garnish with parsley and lemon wedges.

NUTRITIONAL INFO (PER SERVING): Calories: 250 | Protein: 30g | Carbs: 2g | Fats: 12g | Fiber: 0g | Sodium: 150mg

Chicken Marbella with Olives and Capers

Yield: 4 servings
Prep Time: 15 minutes | **Cook Time:** 40 minutes

INGREDIENTS:

- 1.5 lbs chicken thighs
- 1/2 cup green olives, pitted
- 1/4 cup capers, drained
- 1/2 cup prunes, chopped
- 1/4 cup olive oil
- 1/4 cup red wine vinegar
- 2 garlic cloves, minced
- 2 tbsp fresh oregano, chopped
- Salt and pepper, to taste

INSTRUCTIONS:

1. **Marinate Chicken:** Mix olive oil, vinegar, garlic, oregano, salt, and pepper. Add chicken, olives, capers, and prunes; marinate for 30 minutes.
2. **Bake Chicken:** Preheat oven to 375°F (190°C). Bake chicken for 40 minutes, basting occasionally.
3. **Serve:** Garnish with parsley and lemon wedges.

NUTRITIONAL INFO (PER SERVING): Calories: 320 | Protein: 25g | Carbs: 8g | Fats: 20g | Fiber: 2g | Sodium: 450mg

Spiced Meatballs with Tomato Sauce

Yield: 4 servings
Prep Time: 15 minutes | **Cook Time:** 30 minutes

INGREDIENTS:

- 1 lb ground beef or lamb
- 1/4 cup breadcrumbs
- 1/4 cup onion, finely chopped
- 2 garlic cloves, minced
- 1 tsp cumin
- 1 tsp paprika
- Salt and pepper, to taste
- 1 tbsp olive oil

Tomato Sauce:
- 1 can (14 oz) crushed tomatoes
- 1 tbsp olive oil
- 1 garlic clove, minced
- 1 tsp oregano

INSTRUCTIONS:

1. Prepare Meatballs: Mix ground meat, breadcrumbs, onion, garlic, spices, salt, and pepper. Form mixture into balls.

2. Cook Meatballs: Heat olive oil in a skillet over medium heat, cook meatballs until browned on all sides.

3. Make Sauce: In the same skillet, add olive oil, minced garlic, crushed tomatoes, and oregano. Simmer for 5-7 minutes.

4. Combine: Add meatballs to the sauce, cover, and simmer for an additional 15 minutes.

NUTRITIONAL INFO (PER SERVING): Calories: 300 | Protein: 20g | Carbs: 10g | Fats: 18g | Fiber: 2g | Sodium: 400mg

Chicken with Artichokes and Olives

Yield: 4 servings
Prep Time: 10 minutes | **Cook Time:** 20 minutes

INGREDIENTS:

- 1.5 lbs chicken thighs
- 1 cup artichoke hearts, halved
- 1/2 cup green olives, pitted
- 2 garlic cloves, minced
- 2 tbsp olive oil
- 1/2 cup chicken broth
- 1 lemon, juiced
- Fresh herbs (parsley, thyme)
- Salt and pepper, to taste

INSTRUCTIONS:

1. Cook Chicken: Heat olive oil in a large skillet. Sear the chicken thighs about 5 minutes per side. Remove chicken from the skillet.

2. Add Ingredients: In the same skillet, add minced garlic and sauté for 1 minute. Add the artichoke hearts, green olives, chicken broth, and lemon juice. Stir to combine and bring to a simmer. Return the chicken to the skillet, cover, and cook for 15 minutes, or until the chicken is cooked through.

3. Serve: Transfer the chicken and sauce to a serving dish. Garnish with fresh herbs such as parsley and thyme. Serve with lemon wedges on the side for an extra burst of citrus flavor.

NUTRITIONAL INFO (PER SERVING): Calories: 280 | Protein: 24g | Carbohydrates: 5g | Fats: 18g | Fiber: 3g | Sodium: 450mg

Beef Moussaka

Yield: 6 servings
Prep Time: 20 minutes | **Cook Time:** 40 minutes

INGREDIENTS:

- 1 lb ground beef (450 g)
- 2 large eggplants, sliced (600 g)
- 1 onion, chopped (150 g)
- 2 garlic cloves, minced (6 g)
- 1 can (14 oz) crushed tomatoes (400 g)
- 1/2 cup olive oil (120 ml)
- 1 tsp cinnamon (2 g)
- Salt and pepper, to taste

Béchamel Sauce:
- 2 cups milk (480 ml)
- 2 tbsp flour (16 g)
- 2 tbsp butter (30 g)
- 1/4 cup Parmesan cheese, grated (30 g)

INSTRUCTIONS:

1. **Cook Beef:** Sauté onion and garlic in olive oil. Add beef, cook until browned. Add tomatoes, cinnamon, salt, and pepper. Simmer 10 minutes.
2. **Prepare Eggplant:** Brush eggplant slices with olive oil, roast at 400°F (200°C) for 20 minutes.
3. **Make Béchamel:** Melt butter, whisk in flour, slowly add milk, cook until thick. Stir in Parmesan.
4. **Assemble Moussaka:** Layer eggplant, beef, and béchamel in a baking dish. Bake at 350°F (180°C) for 30 minutes.

NUTRITIONAL INFO (PER SERVING): Calories: 320 | Protein: 18g | Carbohydrates: 12g | Fat: 22g | Fiber: 3g | Sodium: 400mg

Grilled Rabbit with Garlic and Herbs

Yield: 4 servings
Prep Time: 10 minutes (plus 30 minutes marinating time) | **Cook Time:** 25 minutes

INGREDIENTS:

- 1 rabbit, cut into pieces (about 1.5 kg)
- 4 garlic cloves, minced (12 g)
- 1 tbsp fresh rosemary, chopped (3 g)
- 2 tbsp olive oil (30 ml)
- 1 tbsp fresh thyme, chopped (3 g)
- Salt and pepper, to taste
- Lemon wedges, for serving (optional)

INSTRUCTIONS:

1. **Marinate Rabbit:** In a large bowl, mix the rabbit pieces with minced garlic, olive oil, chopped fresh rosemary, chopped fresh thyme, salt, and pepper. Cover and refrigerate for at least 30 minutes.
2. **Grill Rabbit:** Preheat the grill to medium heat. Place the marinated rabbit pieces on the grill and cook for 10-12 minutes per side, or until fully cooked and the meat is no longer pink inside.
3. **Serve:** Transfer the grilled rabbit to a serving platter. Garnish with fresh herbs and serve with lemon wedges on the side for added flavor.

NUTRITIONAL INFO (PER SERVING): Calories: 220 | Protein: 30g | Carbohydrates: 0g | Fat: 11g | Fiber: 0g | Sodium: 75mg

Rabbit Bolognese

Yield: 4 servings
Prep Time: 15 minutes | **Cook Time:** 1 hour

INGREDIENTS:

- 1 lb rabbit meat, minced (450 g)
- 1 onion, chopped (150 g)
- 2 garlic cloves, minced (6 g)
- 1 can (14 oz) crushed tomatoes (400 g)
- 1/2 cup carrots, diced (65 g)
- 1/2 cup celery, diced (50 g)
- 1/2 cup white wine (120 ml)
- 2 tbsp olive oil (30 ml)
- 1 tsp oregano (1 g)
- Salt and pepper, to taste
- Fresh basil, chopped (optional, 5 g)
- Parmesan cheese, grated (optional, 20 g)

INSTRUCTIONS:

1. **Sauté Veggies:** Heat olive oil in a skillet, sauté onion, garlic, carrots, and celery until soft.
2. **Cook Rabbit:** Add rabbit, cook until browned. Add wine, simmer 5 minutes.
3. **Add Tomatoes:** Stir in tomatoes, oregano, salt, and pepper. Simmer 45 minutes.
4. **Serve:** Serve pasta topped with basil and Parmesan.

NUTRITIONAL INFO (PER SERVING): Calories: 320 | Protein: 28g | Carbohydrates: 10g | Fat: 18g | Fiber: 3g | Sodium: 300mg

Rabbit with Lemon and Oregano Marinade

Yield: 4 servings
Prep Time: 10 minutes (plus 1 hour marinating time) | **Cook Time:** 30 minutes

INGREDIENTS:

- 1 rabbit, cut into pieces (1 kg)
- 3 tbsp olive oil (45 ml)
- 2 lemons, juiced (60 ml)
- 3 garlic cloves, minced (9 g)
- 2 tbsp fresh oregano, chopped (6 g)
- Salt and pepper, to taste

INSTRUCTIONS:

1. **Marinate Rabbit:** Mix olive oil, lemon juice, minced garlic, chopped oregano, salt, and pepper. Place the rabbit pieces in a shallow dish and pour the marinade over them. Cover and refrigerate for at least 1 hour.
2. **Grill Rabbit:** Preheat a grill to medium heat. Grill the rabbit pieces for about 15 minutes per side, or until the meat is no longer pink. Ensure the meat reaches an internal temperature of 165°F (74°C).
3. **Serve:** Serve garnished with additional fresh oregano and lemon slices.

NUTRITIONAL INFO (PER SERVING): Calories: 230 | Protein: 32g | Carbohydrates: 2g | Fat: 10g | Fiber: 1g | Sodium: 120mg

Rabbit with Wild Mushrooms and Garlic

Yield: 4 servings
Prep Time: 15 minutes | **Cook Time:** 35 minutes

INGREDIENTS:

- 1 rabbit, cut into pieces (1 kg)
- 2 cups wild mushrooms, sliced (200 g)
- 4 garlic cloves, minced (12 g)
- 3 tbsp olive oil (45 ml)
- 1/2 cup chicken broth (120 ml)
- Fresh thyme, chopped (5 g)
- Salt and pepper, to taste

INSTRUCTIONS:

1. **Sauté Rabbit:** Heat olive oil in a skillet over medium heat. Cook the rabbit pieces until browned on all sides, about 5 minutes per side.
2. **Add Mushrooms:** Add the sliced wild mushrooms and minced garlic to the skillet. Cook for about 5 minutes until the mushrooms start to soften and release their juices.
3. **Simmer:** Pour in the chicken broth, add chopped fresh thyme, salt, and pepper. Reduce heat and simmer for 20 minutes, or until the rabbit is fully cooked and tender.

NUTRITIONAL INFO (PER SERVING): Calories: 250 | Protein: 34g | Carbohydrates: 4g | Fat: 10g | Fiber: 1g | Sodium: 150mg

Rabbit with Spinach and Ricotta

Yield: 4 servings
Prep Time: 10 minutes | **Cook Time:** 30 minutes

INGREDIENTS:

- 1 rabbit, cut into pieces (1 kg)
- 2 cups spinach, chopped (60 g)
- 1/2 cup ricotta cheese (125 g)
- 3 garlic cloves, minced (9 g)
- 3 tbsp olive oil (45 ml)
- Salt and pepper, to taste
- Fresh parsley, chopped (5 g)
- Parmesan cheese, grated (optional, 20 g)

INSTRUCTIONS:

1. **Cook Rabbit:** Heat olive oil in a skillet over medium heat. Sauté the rabbit pieces about 10 minutes.
2. **Add Spinach:** Add minced garlic and chopped spinach to the skillet. Cook until the spinach is wilted and fragrant, about 3-4 minutes.
3. **Combine:** Stir in the ricotta cheese, season with salt and pepper, and simmer for 10 minutes until the flavors meld together. Garnish with chopped parsley and optional grated Parmesan cheese.

NUTRITIONAL INFO (PER SERVING): Calories: 260 | Protein: 36g | Carbohydrates: 5g | Fat: 12g | Fiber: 2g | Sodium: 200mg

Rabbit in a Mediterranean Citrus Sauce

Yield: 4 servings
Prep Time: 10 minutes | **Cook Time:** 35 minutes

INGREDIENTS:

- 1 rabbit, cut into pieces (1 kg)
- 1/2 cup orange juice (120 ml)
- 1/4 cup lemon juice (60 ml)
- 2 tbsp olive oil (30 ml)
- 3 garlic cloves, minced (9 g)
- 1 tbsp fresh thyme, chopped (5 g)
- Salt and pepper, to taste
- Orange and lemon slices, for garnish (optional)

INSTRUCTIONS:

1. **Sauté Rabbit:** Heat olive oil in a skillet over medium heat. Cook the rabbit pieces until browned on all sides, about 10 minutes.
2. **Add Sauce:** Add minced garlic, orange juice, lemon juice, fresh thyme, salt, and pepper to the skillet. Bring to a simmer and cook for 25 minutes, or until the rabbit is tender and the sauce is slightly reduced.
3. **Serve:** Garnish with additional citrus slices and fresh thyme. Serve hot.

NUTRITIONAL INFO (PER SERVING): Calories: 240 | Protein: 34g | Carbohydrates: 4g | Fat: 10g | Fiber: 1g | Sodium: 100mg

Rabbit with Mint and Yogurt Sauce

Yield: 4 servings
Prep Time: 10 minutes | **Cook Time:** 30 minutes

INGREDIENTS:

- 1 rabbit, cut into pieces (1 kg)
- 2 tbsp olive oil (30 ml)
- 1 cup Greek yogurt (240 g)
- 2 tbsp fresh mint, chopped (10 g)
- 2 garlic cloves, minced (6 g)
- 1 tbsp lemon juice (15 ml)
- Salt and pepper, to taste

INSTRUCTIONS:

1. **Cook Rabbit:** Heat olive oil in a skillet over medium heat. Sauté the rabbit pieces until browned on all sides, about 10 minutes.
2. **Make Sauce:** In a bowl, mix together Greek yogurt, chopped fresh mint, minced garlic, lemon juice, salt, and pepper until well combined.
3. **Serve:** Plate the cooked rabbit and serve with the mint yogurt sauce. Garnish with additional mint leaves for a fresh finish.

NUTRITIONAL INFO (PER SERVING): Calories: 220 | Protein: 33g | Carbohydrates: 3g | Fat: 9g | Fiber: 0g | Sodium: 80mg

CHAPTER 5: FISH AND SEAFOOD

Roasted Halibut with Mediterranean Vegetables

Yield: 4 servings
Prep Time: 15 minutes | **Cook Time:** 25 minutes

INGREDIENTS:

- 4 halibut fillets (150g each)
- 2 tbsp olive oil (30 ml)
- 1 red bell pepper, sliced (120 g)
- 1 zucchini, sliced (150 g)
- 1 red onion, sliced (100 g)
- 200g cherry tomatoes
- 2 garlic cloves, minced (6 g)
- 1 tsp dried oregano (1g)
- 1 tsp dried thyme (1 g) or fresh, to taste
- 1 lemon, cut into wedges
- Fresh parsley for garnish (optional, 5 g)
- Salt and pepper to taste

INSTRUCTIONS:

1. **Preheat Oven:** Set oven to 400°F (200°C).
2. **Roast Vegetables:** Toss the vegetables with olive oil, garlic, oregano, thyme, salt, and pepper. Roast for 15 minutes.
3. **Cook Halibut:** Season halibut with salt and pepper; place on top of vegetables. Roast for 10-12 more minutes.
4. **Serve:** Garnish with parsley and lemon wedges.

NUTRITIONAL INFO (PER SERVING): Calories: 280 | Protein: 32g | Carbohydrates: 10g | Fat: 12g | Fiber: 3g | Sodium: 320mg

Mediterranean Baked Cod

Yield: 4 servings
Prep Time: 10 minutes | **Cook Time:** 20 minutes

INGREDIENTS:

- 4 cod fillets (about 600 g)
- 1 cup cherry tomatoes, halved (150 g)
- 1/2 cup Kalamata olives, pitted (75 g)
- 2 garlic cloves, minced (6 g)
- 2 tbsp olive oil (30 ml)
- 1 tbsp fresh oregano, chopped (5 g)
- Lemon slices, for garnish (optional)
- Salt and pepper, to taste

INSTRUCTIONS:

1. **Prepare Cod:** Preheat the oven to 375°F (190°C). Place the cod fillets in a baking dish.
2. **Add Toppings:** Spread cherry tomatoes, olives, garlic, and oregano over the cod fillets. Drizzle the dish with olive oil and season with salt and pepper.
3. **Bake:** Bake the dish for about 20 minutes.
4. **Serve:** Garnish the baked cod with fresh lemon slices and a sprinkle of parsley, if desired.

NUTRITIONAL INFO (PER SERVING): Calories: 210 | Protein: 30g | Carbohydrates: 3g | Fat: 8g | Fiber: 1g | Sodium: 300mg

Tuna Steaks with Caper Relish

Yield: 4 servings
Prep Time: 10 minutes | **Cook Time:** 8 minutes

INGREDIENTS:

- 4 tuna steaks (about 600 g)
- 2 tbsp olive oil (30 ml)
- 1/4 cup capers, rinsed (35 g)
- 1/4 cup Kalamata olives, chopped (35 g)
- 1/2 cup cherry tomatoes, chopped (75 g)
- 2 tbsp fresh parsley, chopped (5 g)
- 1 tbsp lemon juice (15 ml)
- Salt and pepper, to taste

INSTRUCTIONS:

1. **Sear Tuna:** Heat olive oil in a skillet over medium-high heat. Season the tuna steaks with salt and pepper. Sear each side for 2-3 minutes, or until the tuna is cooked to your liking.
2. **Prepare Relish:** Mix together capers, chopped Kalamata olives, chopped cherry tomatoes, fresh parsley, lemon juice, salt, and pepper to make the relish.
3. **Serve:** Top each tuna steak with a generous amount of caper relish. Garnish with lemon wedges and serve immediately.

NUTRITIONAL INFO (PER SERVING): Calories: 240 | Protein: 35g | Carbohydrates: 3g | Fat: 10g | Fiber: 1g | Sodium: 400mg

Grilled Swordfish with Olive Tapenade

Yield: 4 servings
Prep Time: 10 minutes | **Cook Time:** 10 minutes

INGREDIENTS:

- 4 swordfish steaks (about 600 g)
- 2 tbsp olive oil (30 ml)
- 1/2 cup black olives, pitted (75 g)
- 2 tbsp capers, rinsed (20 g)
- 1 garlic clove, minced (3 g)
- 1 tbsp fresh parsley, chopped (5 g)
- 1 tbsp lemon juice (15 ml)
- Salt and pepper, to taste

INSTRUCTIONS:

1. **Grill Swordfish:** Brush the swordfish steaks with olive oil and season with salt and pepper. Preheat the grill to medium-high heat and grill the steaks for 4-5 minutes per side, or until fully cooked.
2. **Make Tapenade:** In a food processor, blend the black olives, capers, minced garlic, fresh parsley, and lemon juice until smooth to create the tapenade.
3. **Serve:** Top the grilled swordfish steaks with the olive tapenade and garnish with lemon wedges. Serve hot.

NUTRITIONAL INFO (PER SERVING): Calories: 280 | Protein: 36g | Carbohydrates: 2g | Fat: 14g | Fiber: 1g | Sodium: 350mg

Herb-Crusted Baked Trout

Yield: 4 servings
Prep Time: 10 minutes | **Cook Time:** 20 minutes

INGREDIENTS:

- 4 trout fillets (600 g)
- 1/2 cup breadcrumbs (50 g)
- 2 tbsp fresh parsley, chopped (5 g)
- 1 tbsp fresh dill, chopped (3 g)
- 2 garlic cloves, minced (6 g)
- 2 tbsp olive oil (30 ml)
- Lemon wedges, for serving
- Salt and pepper, to taste

INSTRUCTIONS:

1. **Prepare Topping:** In a bowl, mix breadcrumbs, chopped parsley, chopped dill, minced garlic, olive oil, salt, and pepper to create the herb topping.
2. **Bake Trout:** Preheat the oven to 375°F (190°C). Place the trout fillets on a baking sheet and top each fillet with the herb mixture. Bake for 15-20 minutes or until the trout is cooked through, and the topping is golden brown.
3. **Serve:** Garnish the baked trout with lemon wedges and additional fresh herbs before serving. Serve immediately.

NUTRITIONAL INFO (PER SERVING): Calories: 250 | Protein: 28g | Carbohydrates: 5g | Fat: 12g | Fiber: 1g | Sodium: 150mg

Mussels in White Wine Sauce

Yield: 4 servings
Prep Time: 10 minutes | **Cook Time:** 15 minutes

INGREDIENTS:

- 2 lbs mussels, cleaned (900 g)
- 1/2 cup white wine (120 ml)
- 2 tbsp olive oil (30 ml)
- 1 onion, finely chopped (150 g)
- 3 garlic cloves, minced (9 g)
- 2 tbsp fresh parsley, chopped (5 g)
- Salt and pepper, to taste
- Lemon wedges, for serving

INSTRUCTIONS:

1. **Sauté Aromatics:** Heat olive oil in a large skillet over medium heat. Sauté the chopped onion and minced garlic for about 3 minutes until fragrant.
2. **Cook Mussels:** Add the cleaned mussels, white wine, salt, and pepper to the skillet. Cover and cook for 5-7 minutes, or until the mussels open. Discard any mussels that do not open.
3. **Serve:** Garnish with chopped parsley and serve with lemon wedges. Enjoy with crusty bread if desired.

NUTRITIONAL INFO (PER SERVING): Calories: 180 | Protein: 20g | Carbohydrates: 4g | Fat: 8g | Fiber: 1g | Sodium: 300mg

Sardines with Lemon and Parsley

Yield: 4 servings
Prep Time: 5 minutes | **Cook Time:** 10 minutes

INGREDIENTS:

- 8 sardines, cleaned (600 g)
- 2 tbsp olive oil (30 ml)
- 2 tbsp fresh parsley, chopped (5 g)
- 2 tbsp lemon juice (30 ml)
- Salt and pepper, to taste
- Lemon wedges, for serving

INSTRUCTIONS:

1. **Prepare Sardines:** Pat the sardines dry with a paper towel. Brush each sardine with olive oil, coating both sides evenly. Season with salt and pepper to taste.
2. **Grill Sardines:** Preheat your grill to medium heat. Place the sardines on the grill and cook for about 3-4 minutes on each side, or until fully cooked with a nice char. The flesh should be opaque and flake easily with a fork.
3. **Serve:** Transfer the grilled sardines to a serving platter. Drizzle with fresh lemon juice and sprinkle with chopped parsley. Serve immediately with lemon wedges on the side for extra flavor.

NUTRITIONAL INFO (PER SERVING): Calories: 150 | Protein: 18g | Carbohydrates: 0g | Fat: 9g | Fiber: 0g | Sodium: 180mg

Salmon Cakes with Dill Sauce

Yield: 4 servings
Prep Time: 10 minutes | **Cook Time:** 15 minutes

INGREDIENTS:

- 1 lb salmon, cooked and flaked (450 g)
- 1/2 cup breadcrumbs (60 g)
- 1/4 cup onion, finely chopped (40 g)
- 1 egg, beaten (50 g)
- 2 tbsp fresh dill, chopped (5 g)
- 1 tbsp lemon juice (15 ml)
- 2 tbsp olive oil (30 ml)

Dill Sauce:
- 1/2 cup Greek yogurt (120 g)
- 1 tbsp fresh dill, chopped (5 g)
- 1 tbsp lemon juice (15 ml)
- Salt and pepper, to taste

INSTRUCTIONS:

1. **Make Cakes:** Mix salmon, breadcrumbs, onion, egg, dill, and lemon juice in a bowl. Form the mixture into patties.
2. **Cook Cakes:** Heat olive oil in a skillet over medium heat. Cook the patties for 3-4 minutes per side or until golden brown.
3. **Serve:** Combine Greek yogurt, dill, lemon juice, salt, and pepper to make the dill sauce. Serve the salmon cakes topped with the dill sauce and garnish with fresh dill and lemon wedges.

NUTRITIONAL INFO (PER SERVING): Calories: 260 | Protein: 28g | Carbohydrates: 8g | Fat: 12g | Fiber: 1g | Sodium: 220mg

Baked Sea Bass with Tomatoes

Yield: 4 servings
Prep Time: 10 minutes | **Cook Time:** 25 minutes

INGREDIENTS:

- 1 whole sea bass, cleaned (about 800 g)
- 1 cup cherry tomatoes, halved (150 g)
- 3 garlic cloves, minced (9 g)
- 2 tbsp olive oil (30 ml)
- 1 tbsp fresh parsley, chopped (5 g)
- 1 tbsp lemon juice (15 ml)
- Salt and pepper, to taste
- Lemon wedges, for serving

INSTRUCTIONS:

1. **Prepare Sea Bass:** Preheat your oven to 375°F (190°C). Rinse and pat dry the sea bass, then place it in a baking dish.
2. **Add Toppings:** Arrange the halved cherry tomatoes and minced garlic around the fish. Drizzle the sea bass and tomatoes with olive oil and lemon juice. Season generously with salt and pepper.
3. **Bake the Fish:** Place the dish in the oven and bake for 25 minutes, or until the sea bass is opaque and flakes easily when tested with a fork. The tomatoes should be soft and slightly caramelized.
4. **Serve:** Garnish the baked sea bass with fresh parsley and serve immediately with lemon wedges

NUTRITIONAL INFO (PER SERVING): Calories: 240 | Protein: 30g | Carbohydrates: 3g | Fat: 12g | Fiber: 1g | Sodium: 180mg

Garlic Shrimp with Lemon Butter

Yield: 4 servings
Prep Time: 5 minutes | **Cook Time:** 10 minutes

INGREDIENTS:

- 1 lb shrimp, peeled and deveined (450 g)
- 3 tbsp butter (45 g)
- 4 garlic cloves, minced (12 g)
- 2 tbsp lemon juice (30 ml)
- Fresh parsley, chopped (5 g)
- Salt and pepper, to taste
- Lemon slices, for serving

INSTRUCTIONS:

1. **Sauté Shrimp:** In a large skillet over medium heat, melt the butter. Add the minced garlic and cook for about 1 minute, stirring frequently.
2. **Cook Shrimp:** Add the shrimp to the skillet in a single layer. Cook for about 3-4 minutes, turning halfway through, until the shrimp turn pink.
3. **Add Lemon and Season:** Stir in the lemon juice, and season the shrimp with salt and pepper. Let it simmer for an additional 2 minutes.
4. **Serve:** Transfer the shrimp to a serving dish, garnish with chopped parsley, and serve with lemon slices.

NUTRITIONAL INFO (PER SERVING): Calories: 210 | Protein: 20g | Carbohydrates: 1g | Fat: 14g | Fiber: 0g | Sodium: 320mg

Grilled Mackerel with Herbs

Yield: 4 servings
Prep Time: 10 minutes | **Cook Time:** 15 minutes

INGREDIENTS:

- 4 whole mackerel, cleaned (about 1.2 kg)
- 2 tbsp olive oil (30 ml)
- 2 tbsp fresh herbs (rosemary, thyme), chopped (10 g)
- 1 lemon, sliced (120 g)
- Salt and pepper, to taste
- Fresh parsley, for garnish (5 g)

INSTRUCTIONS:

1. **Prepare Mackerel:** Rub the cleaned mackerel with olive oil, chopped herbs, salt, and pepper. Stuff each fish with lemon slices for extra flavor.
2. **Grill Fish:** Preheat the grill to medium heat. Grill the mackerel for 6-7 minutes per side, or until cooked through and slightly charred on the outside.
3. **Serve:** Garnish with fresh parsley and extra lemon wedges. Serve immediately.

NUTRITIONAL INFO (PER SERVING): Calories: 250 | Protein: 32g | Carbohydrates: 1g | Fat: 12g | Fiber: 0g | Sodium: 220mg

Grilled Fish Kebabs

Yield: 4 servings
Prep Time: 10 minutes | **Cook Time:** 15 minutes

INGREDIENTS:

- 1 lb fish fillets, cubed (450 g)
- 1 bell pepper, chopped (120 g)
- 1 red onion, chopped (100 g)
- 1 cup cherry tomatoes (150 g)
- 2 tbsp olive oil (30 ml)
- 1 tbsp lemon juice (15 ml)
- Fresh herbs (parsley, thyme), chopped (10 g)
- Salt and pepper, to taste

INSTRUCTIONS:

1. **Prepare Skewers:** Thread the cubed fish, chopped bell pepper, chopped red onion, and cherry tomatoes onto skewers.
2. **Season:** Drizzle the skewers with olive oil and lemon juice. Sprinkle with chopped fresh herbs, salt, and pepper.
3. **Grill Kebabs:** Preheat the grill to medium heat. Grill the kebabs for 3-4 minutes per side, or until the fish is opaque and cooked through.
4. **Serve:** Serve hot, garnished with additional herbs if desired.

NUTRITIONAL INFO (PER SERVING): Calories: 200 | Protein: 24g | Carbohydrates: 4g | Fat: 10g | Fiber: 1g | Sodium: 180mg

Stuffed Squid with Rice and Herbs

Yield: 4 servings
Prep Time: 15 minutes | **Cook Time:** 30 minutes

INGREDIENTS:

- 8 squid tubes, cleaned (about 600 g)
- 1 cup cooked rice (200 g)
- 2 tbsp olive oil (30 ml)
- 1/4 cup onion, chopped (30 g)
- 2 garlic cloves, minced (6 g)
- 2 tbsp fresh parsley, chopped (5 g)
- 1 tbsp fresh mint, chopped (2 g)
- 1 tbsp lemon juice (15 ml)
- Salt and pepper, to taste

INSTRUCTIONS:

1. **Prepare Filling:** Sauté onion and garlic in olive oil until softened. Mix with cooked rice, parsley, mint, lemon juice, salt, and pepper.
2. **Stuff Squid:** Fill each squid tube with the rice mixture and secure the ends with toothpicks to prevent filling from falling out.
3. **Cook Squid:** Heat olive oil in a skillet, place the stuffed squid in the pan, and cook for 10-12 minutes, turning occasionally, until the squid is tender and fully cooked.

NUTRITIONAL INFO (PER SERVING): Calories: 220 | Protein: 18g | Carbohydrates: 16g | Fat: 8g | Fiber: 1g | Sodium: 140mg

Shrimp Skewers with Spicy Yogurt Sauce

Yield: 4 servings
Prep Time: 10 minutes | **Cook Time:** 10 minutes

INGREDIENTS:

- 1 lb shrimp, peeled and deveined (450 g)
- 2 tbsp olive oil (30 ml)
- 1 tsp paprika (2 g)
- 1 tsp cayenne pepper (2 g)
- Salt and pepper, to taste

Spicy Yogurt Sauce:
- 1/2 cup Greek yogurt (120 g)
- 1 tbsp lemon juice (15 ml)
- 1 tsp hot sauce (5 ml)
- 1 tbsp fresh cilantro, chopped (5 g)

INSTRUCTIONS:

1. **Prepare Shrimp:** Toss shrimp with olive oil, paprika, cayenne, salt, and pepper.
2. **Grill Skewers:** Thread shrimp onto skewers. Preheat grill to medium heat and grill skewers for 3-4 minutes per side.
3. **Make Sauce:** In a small bowl, mix yogurt, lemon juice, hot sauce, and cilantro until smooth.
4. **Serve:** Plate the grilled shrimp skewers and serve with the spicy yogurt sauce on the side. Garnish with additional herbs if desired.

NUTRITIONAL INFO (PER SERVING): Calories: 220 | Protein: 24g | Carbohydrates: 3g | Fat: 12g | Fiber: 0g | Sodium: 250mg

Saffron Shrimp Risotto

Yield: 4 servings
Prep Time: 10 minutes | **Cook Time:** 25 minutes

INGREDIENTS:

- 1 lb shrimp, peeled (450 g)
- 1 cup Arborio rice (200 g)
- 4 cups chicken broth (960 ml)
- 1/2 cup white wine (120 ml)
- 1/2 onion, chopped (75 g)
- 2 garlic cloves, minced (6 g)
- 1 pinch saffron threads (0.1 g)
- 2 tbsp olive oil (30 ml)
- Salt and pepper, to taste
- Fresh parsley, chopped (5 g)

INSTRUCTIONS:

1. **Sauté Onion:** Heat olive oil in a skillet over medium heat. Sauté onion and garlic 3 minutes.
2. **Add Rice and Saffron:** Stir in Arborio rice and saffron threads, cooking for 1 minute. Add white wine and simmer until absorbed.
3. **Cook Risotto:** Gradually add chicken broth, stirring constantly until each addition is absorbed. Continue until the rice is creamy, about 20 minutes.
4. **Add Shrimp:** Stir in shrimp and cook until pink and opaque, about 4-5 minutes. Season with salt and pepper.
5. **Serve:** Garnish with chopped parsley and a sprinkle of lemon zest.

NUTRITIONAL INFO (PER SERVING): Calories: 320 | Protein: 20g | Carbohydrates: 40g | Fat: 10g | Fiber: 1g | Sodium: 350mg

Baked Clams with Oregano and Lemon

Yield: 4 servings
Prep Time: 10 minutes | **Cook Time:** 15 minutes

INGREDIENTS:

- 2 dozen clams, cleaned (about 1 kg)
- 1/2 cup breadcrumbs (60 g)
- 2 tbsp olive oil (30 ml)
- 1 tsp oregano (1 g)
- 2 garlic cloves, minced (6 g)
- 1 tbsp lemon juice (15 ml)
- Fresh parsley, chopped (5 g)
- Salt and pepper, to taste

INSTRUCTIONS:

1. **Prepare Topping:** In a bowl, mix together breadcrumbs, olive oil, oregano, garlic, lemon juice, salt, and pepper until well combined.
2. **Bake Clams:** Preheat oven to 375°F (190°C). Arrange clams on a baking sheet. Spoon breadcrumb mixture over each clam. Bake for 10-12 minutes, or until breadcrumbs are golden brown and clams are cooked through.
3. **Serve:** Garnish with freshly chopped parsley and serve with lemon wedges on the side.

NUTRITIONAL INFO (PER SERVING): Calories: 180 | Protein: 15g | Carbohydrates: 10g | Fat: 8g | Fiber: 1g | Sodium: 290mg

Tuna Tartare with Avocado

Yield: 4 servings
Prep Time: 15 minutes | **Cook Time:** None

INGREDIENTS:

- 1 lb fresh tuna, diced (450 g)
- 2 avocados, diced (300 g)
- 2 tbsp lime juice (30 ml)
- 1 tbsp sesame oil (15 ml)
- 1 tbsp soy sauce (15 ml)
- 1 tbsp sesame seeds (10 g)
- Fresh herbs (cilantro, mint), chopped (10 g)
- Salt and pepper, to taste

INSTRUCTIONS:

1. **Mix Ingredients:** In a medium bowl, gently combine the diced fresh tuna and avocados. Add the lime juice, sesame oil, and soy sauce, then season with salt and pepper. Be careful to toss gently, so the avocado stays intact and doesn't become mushy.
2. **Serve:** Divide the tuna tartare mixture evenly among individual serving plates. Garnish each portion with a sprinkle of sesame seeds and a handful of freshly chopped herbs like cilantro and mint for a fresh burst of flavor.
3. **Presentation Tip:** Serve the tartare with some extra lime wedges, and enjoy immediately while the ingredients are fresh.

NUTRITIONAL INFO (PER SERVING): Calories: 220 | Protein: 25g | Carbohydrates: 6g | Fat: 12g | Fiber: 3g | Sodium: 250mg

Seafood Paella

Yield: 4 servings
Prep Time: 15 minutes | **Cook Time:** 30 minutes

INGREDIENTS:

- 1 cup Arborio rice (200 g)
- 2 cups seafood stock (480 ml)
- 1/2 cup white wine (120 ml)
- 1/2 lb shrimp (peeled), mussels and clams (cleaned), calamari (sliced) (225 g each)
- 1/2 cup peas (75 g)
- 1 onion, chopped (150 g)
- 1 bell pepper, chopped (120g)
- 3 garlic cloves, minced (9g)
- 1 tsp saffron threads (0.5g)
- 2 tbsp olive oil (30 ml)
- Salt and pepper, to taste
- Fresh parsley, chopped (10 g)

INSTRUCTIONS:

1. **Sauté Veggies:** Heat olive oil in a large skillet or paella pan over medium heat. Sauté onion, garlic, and bell pepper until soft.
2. **Add Rice and Saffron:** Stir in Arborio rice and saffron, cooking for 1 minute. Add white wine, simmer until absorbed.
3. **Cook Paella:** Add seafood stock, shrimp, mussels, clams, and calamari. Simmer until the rice and the seafood are cooked, about 20 minutes.
4. **Serve:** Garnish with peas, fresh parsley, and lemon wedges.

NUTRITIONAL INFO (PER SERVING): Calories: 380 | Protein: 30g | Carbohydrates: 40g | Fat: 12g | Fiber: 3g | Sodium: 400mg

Prawn and Mango Salad

Yield: 4 servings
Prep Time: 10 minutes | **Cook Time:** None

INGREDIENTS:

- 1 lb prawns, cooked (450 g)
- 1 mango, diced (200 g)
- 1 avocado, diced (150 g)
- 1 cup cherry tomatoes, halved (150 g)
- 4 cups mixed greens (120 g)
- 2 tbsp lime juice (30 ml)
- 1 tbsp olive oil (15 ml)
- Fresh cilantro, chopped (10 g)
- Salt and pepper, to taste

INSTRUCTIONS:

1. **Combine:** In a large bowl, toss cooked prawns, mango, avocado, cherry tomatoes, and mixed greens together.
2. **Dress:** Drizzle with lime juice and olive oil. Season with salt and pepper to taste. Toss gently to coat evenly.
3. **Serve:** Garnish with freshly chopped cilantro and serve immediately.

NUTRITIONAL INFO (PER SERVING): Calories: 200 | Protein: 18g | Carbohydrates: 15g | Fat: 10g | Fiber: 5g | Sodium: 150mg

Cod Fillets with Lemon and Capers

Yield: 4 servings
Prep Time: 5 minutes | **Cook Time:** 15 minutes

INGREDIENTS:

- 4 cod fillets (600 g)
- 2 tbsp olive oil (30 ml)
- 2 tbsp lemon juice (30 ml)
- 2 tbsp capers, rinsed (20 g)
- 2 garlic cloves, minced (6 g)
- Fresh parsley, chopped (10 g)
- Salt and pepper, to taste

INSTRUCTIONS:

1. **Sauté Cod:** Heat olive oil in a skillet over medium heat. Season cod fillets with salt and pepper. Sauté each fillet for 3-4 minutes per side, or until golden and cooked through.
2. **Add Sauce:** Add minced garlic, lemon juice, and rinsed capers to the skillet. Cook for an additional 2 minutes, allowing the flavors to blend.
3. **Serve:** Garnish cod fillets with freshly chopped parsley and serve with lemon slices on the side.

NUTRITIONAL INFO (PER SERVING): Calories: 180 | Protein: 28g | Carbohydrates: 2g | Fat: 8g | Fiber: 0g | Sodium: 220mg

CHAPTER 6: VEGETABLES AND SIDES

Grilled Asparagus with Lemon

Yield: 4 servings
Prep Time: 5 minutes | **Cook Time:** 8 minutes

INGREDIENTS:

- 1 lb asparagus, trimmed (450 g)
- 2 tbsp olive oil (30 ml)
- 1 tbsp lemon juice (15 ml)
- Salt and pepper, to taste
- Lemon zest and parsley, for garnish (optional, 5 g)

INSTRUCTIONS:

1. **Prepare Asparagus:** In a large bowl, toss the trimmed asparagus with olive oil, lemon juice, salt, and pepper, ensuring they are well coated.
2. **Grill:** Preheat a grill to medium heat. Place the asparagus on the grill and cook for about 3-4 minutes per side, turning occasionally until they are tender and have grill marks.
3. **Serve:** Transfer to a serving plate and garnish with fresh lemon zest and chopped parsley for a burst of freshness and flavor. Enjoy immediately.

NUTRITIONAL INFO (PER SERVING): Calories: 70 | Protein: 2g | Carbohydrates: 5g | Fat: 5g | Fiber: 2g | Sodium: 40mg

Zucchini Fritters with Tzatziki

Yield: 4 servings
Prep Time: 10 minutes | **Cook Time:** 15 minutes

INGREDIENTS:

- 2 zucchinis, grated (300 g)
- 1/2 cup flour (60 g)
- 1 egg, beaten (50 g)
- 2 tbsp fresh dill, chopped (5 g)
- 1/2 tsp salt (2 g)
- 2 tbsp olive oil (30 ml)

Tzatziki:
- 1/2 cup Greek yogurt (120 g)
- 1/2 cucumber, grated (75 g)
- 1 garlic clove, minced (3 g)
- 1 tbsp lemon juice (15 ml)
- Salt and pepper, to taste

INSTRUCTIONS:

1. **Prepare Fritters:** Mix grated zucchini, flour, beaten egg, dill, and salt in a bowl. Form the mixture into small patties.
2. **Cook Fritters:** Heat olive oil in a skillet over medium heat. Fry the patties for 3-4 minutes.
3. **Make Tzatziki:** In a separate bowl, combine Greek yogurt, grated cucumber, minced garlic, lemon juice, and season with salt and pepper.
4. **Serve:** Serve the zucchini fritters warm, alongside the tzatziki, and garnish with fresh dill.

NUTRITIONAL INFO (PER SERVING): Calories: 150 | Protein: 5g | Carbohydrates: 12g | Fat: 9g | Fiber: 2g | Sodium: 180mg

Stuffed Grape Leaves with Rice

Yield: 4 servings
Prep Time: 20 minutes | **Cook Time:** 30 minutes

INGREDIENTS:

- 20 grape leaves, rinsed (200 g)
- 1 cup rice, cooked (180 g)
- 1/2 cup onion, chopped (75g)
- 2 tbsp olive oil (30 ml)
- 2 tbsp pine nuts (15 g)
- 2 tbsp fresh mint, chopped (5 g)
- 2 tbsp fresh parsley, chopped (5 g)
- 1 tbsp lemon juice (15 ml)
- 2 cups vegetable or chicken broth
- Salt and pepper, to taste

INSTRUCTIONS:

1. **Prepare Filling:** In a bowl, mix the cooked rice, chopped onion, olive oil, pine nuts, fresh mint, parsley, lemon juice, salt, and pepper until combined.
2. **Stuff Leaves:** Lay a grape leaf flat with the vein side up. Place a spoonful of filling near the stem end. Fold the sides over the filling, then roll up tightly. Repeat for the remaining leaves.
3. **Cook:** Arrange the stuffed leaves seam-side down in a pot. Pour broth to cover them, place a small plate on top to keep them submerged, and simmer for 30 minutes.

NUTRITIONAL INFO (PER SERVING): Calories: 180 | Protein: 4g | Carbohydrates: 26g | Fats: 7g | Fiber: 3g | Sodium: 180mg

Roasted Cauliflower with Tahini Sauce

Yield: 4 servings
Prep Time: 5 minutes | **Cook Time:** 25 minutes

INGREDIENTS:

- 1 head cauliflower, cut into florets (600 g)
- 2 tbsp olive oil (30 ml)
- Salt and pepper, to taste

Tahini Sauce:
- 1/4 cup tahini (60 g)
- 2 tbsp lemon juice (30 ml)
- 1 garlic clove, minced (3 g)
- 2–3 tbsp water, to adjust consistency
- Salt, to taste

INSTRUCTIONS:

1. **Roast Cauliflower:** Preheat the oven to 400°F (200°C). Toss the cauliflower florets with olive oil, salt, and pepper. Spread them evenly on a baking sheet and roast for 25 minutes, flipping halfway through, until golden and tender.
2. **Prepare Sauce:** In a bowl, combine tahini, lemon juice, minced garlic, water, and salt. Mix until smooth and creamy, adding more water for a pourable consistency if needed.
3. **Serve:** Drizzle the tahini sauce over the roasted cauliflower. Garnish with chopped parsley and sesame seeds for added flavor and texture.

NUTRITIONAL INFO (PER SERVING): Calories: 120 | Protein: 4g | Carbohydrates: 10g | Fats: 8g | Fiber: 3g | Sodium: 70mg

Mediterranean Quinoa Pilaf

Yield: 4 servings
Prep Time: 10 minutes | **Cook Time:** 20 minutes

INGREDIENTS:

- 1 cup quinoa, rinsed (180 g)
- 2 cups vegetable broth (480 ml)
- 1 bell pepper, chopped (150 g)
- 1/2 cup cherry tomatoes, halved (75 g)
- 1/4 cup red onion, chopped (40 g)
- 2 tbsp olive oil (30 ml)
- 2 tbsp fresh parsley, chopped (5 g)
- 1 tbsp lemon juice (15ml)
- Salt and pepper, to taste

INSTRUCTIONS:

1. **Cook Quinoa:** In a pot, combine the quinoa and vegetable broth. Bring to a boil, then reduce to a simmer and cook for 15 minutes or until all the liquid is absorbed. Fluff with a fork and set aside.
2. **Sauté Veggies:** Heat olive oil in a skillet over medium heat. Sauté the bell pepper, cherry tomatoes, and red onion for 5-7 minutes.
3. **Combine:** Add the sautéed vegetables to the cooked quinoa, along with the lemon juice, salt, and pepper. Toss to combine.
4. **Serve:** Garnish with chopped parsley before serving.

NUTRITIONAL INFO (PER SERVING): Calories: 200 | Protein: 5g | Carbohydrates: 30g | Fats: 7g | Fiber: 4g | Sodium: 180mg

Lentil Pilaf with Caramelized Onions

Yield: 4 servings
Prep Time: 10 minutes | **Cook Time:** 30 minutes

INGREDIENTS:

- 1 cup lentils, rinsed (200 g)
- 1/2 cup basmati rice (90 g)
- 2 onions, thinly sliced (200 g)
- 2 cups vegetable broth (480 ml)
- 3 tbsp olive oil (45 ml)
- 1 tsp cumin (2 g)
- Salt and pepper, to taste
- Fresh parsley, for garnish (optional, 5 g)

INSTRUCTIONS:

1. **Caramelize Onions:** Heat 2 tbsp of olive oil in a skillet over low heat. Add the sliced onions and cook slowly for about 15 minutes, stirring occasionally until golden brown and caramelized.
2. **Cook Lentils and Rice:** In a pot, heat 1 tbsp of olive oil over medium heat. Add cumin, lentils, rice, vegetable broth, salt, and pepper. Bring to a boil, then reduce to a simmer and cook for 20 minutes or until the lentils and rice are tender and the liquid is absorbed.
3. **Combine:** Fluff the lentil and rice mixture with a fork. Top with caramelized onions and garnish with fresh parsley before serving.

NUTRITIONAL INFO (PER SERVING): Calories: 220 | Protein: 8g | Carbohydrates: 34g | Fats: 7g | Fiber: 8g | Sodium: 150mg

Mediterranean Stuffed Tomatoes

Yield: 4 servings
Prep Time: 10 minutes | **Cook Time:** 25 minutes

INGREDIENTS:

- 4 large tomatoes, tops removed and scooped (600 g)
- 1 cup quinoa, cooked (180 g)
- 1/2 cup feta cheese, crumbled (75 g)
- 1/4 cup fresh parsley, chopped (15 g)
- 1/4 cup breadcrumbs (30g)
- 2 tbsp olive oil (30 ml)
- Salt and pepper, to taste

INSTRUCTIONS:

1. **Prepare Filling:** In a bowl, mix cooked quinoa, feta cheese, chopped parsley, salt, and pepper until well combined.
2. **Stuff Tomatoes:** Spoon the quinoa mixture into each tomato, filling them generously. Top with breadcrumbs and drizzle with 1 tbsp olive oil.
3. **Bake:** Place the stuffed tomatoes in a baking dish, drizzle with olive oil, and bake at 375°F (190°C) for 25 minutes or until the tomatoes are tender and the tops are golden brown.

NUTRITIONAL INFO (PER SERVING): Calories: 180 | Protein: 6g | Carbohydrates: 20g | Fats: 8g | Fiber: 5g | Sodium: 180mg

Garlic Green Beans with Almonds

Yield: 4 servings
Prep Time: 5 minutes | **Cook Time:** 10 minutes

INGREDIENTS:

- 1 lb green beans, trimmed (450 g)
- 3 garlic cloves, minced (9 g)
- 2 tbsp olive oil (30 ml)
- 1/4 cup almonds, sliced (30 g)
- 1 tsp lemon zest (2 g)
- Salt and pepper, to taste

INSTRUCTIONS:

1. **Sauté Beans:** Heat olive oil in a large skillet over medium heat. Add green beans and minced garlic, sauté for 5-7 minutes until beans are tender and garlic is fragrant.
2. **Add Almonds:** Stir in sliced almonds, cook for another 2-3 minutes until the almonds are lightly toasted and beans are fully tender.
3. **Serve:** Remove from heat and garnish with lemon zest. Serve warm.

NUTRITIONAL INFO (PER SERVING): Calories: 110 | Protein: 3g | Carbohydrates: 8g | Fats: 8g | Fiber: 4g | Sodium: 40mg

Marinated Grilled Vegetables

Yield: 4 servings
Prep Time: 10 minutes | **Cook Time:** 15 minutes

INGREDIENTS:

- 1 zucchini, sliced (150 g)
- 1 bell pepper, sliced (120 g)
- 1 eggplant, sliced (250 g)
- 1 cup cherry tomatoes (150 g)
- 3 tbsp olive oil (45 ml)
- 2 garlic cloves, minced (6g)
- 1 tbsp fresh oregano, chopped (5 g)
- Salt and pepper, to taste

INSTRUCTIONS:

1. **Marinate Vegetables:** In a large bowl, mix olive oil, garlic, oregano, salt, and pepper. Add the sliced zucchini, bell pepper, eggplant, and cherry tomatoes, tossing to coat evenly. Let them marinate for about 10 minutes to absorb the flavors.
2. **Grill:** Preheat a grill or grill pan over medium-high heat. Grill the marinated vegetables for 5-7 minutes on each side, until they are tender and slightly charred.
3. **Serve:** Arrange grilled vegetables on a serving platter and drizzle with any remaining marinade. Serve warm or at room temperature.

NUTRITIONAL INFO (PER SERVING): Calories: 130 | Protein: 2g | Carbohydrates: 10g | Fats: 10g | Fiber: 4g | Sodium: 50mg

Braised Artichokes with Lemon

Yield: 4 servings
Prep Time: 10 minutes | **Cook Time:** 25 minutes

INGREDIENTS:

- 4 artichokes, trimmed (600 g)
- 2 tbsp olive oil (30 ml)
- 1 lemon, juiced and zested (60 ml juice, 5 g zest)
- 2 garlic cloves, minced (6 g)
- 1 cup vegetable broth (240 ml)
- Salt and pepper, to taste
- Fresh herbs (parsley or thyme), for garnish (5 g)

INSTRUCTIONS:

1. **Sauté Artichokes:** Heat olive oil in a large skillet over medium heat. Add the artichokes, garlic, salt, and pepper. Sauté for 5-7 minutes until the artichokes start to brown.
2. **Braise:** Pour in the vegetable broth, lemon juice, and zest. Cover the skillet and simmer for 20 minutes, or until the artichokes are tender and have absorbed the flavors.
3. **Serve:** Transfer the braised artichokes to a serving dish and garnish with fresh herbs. Serve warm.

NUTRITIONAL INFO (PER SERVING): Calories: 120 | Protein: 2g | Carbohydrates: 12g | Fats: 7g | Fiber: 6g | Sodium: 140mg

Chickpea and Spinach Stew

Yield: 4 servings
Prep Time: 10 minutes | **Cook Time:** 20 minutes

INGREDIENTS:

- 1 can (15 oz) chickpeas, drained (425 g)
- 2 cups spinach, chopped (60 g)
- 1 can (14 oz) diced tomatoes (400 g)
- 1 onion, chopped (150 g)
- 2 garlic cloves, minced (6g)
- 2 tbsp olive oil (30 ml)
- 1 tsp cumin (2 g)
- Salt and pepper, to taste
- Fresh herbs (parsley or cilantro), for garnish (5 g)

INSTRUCTIONS:

1. **Sauté Base:** In a large skillet, heat olive oil over medium heat. Add chopped onion and minced garlic, sautéing until the onion is translucent and fragrant, about 5 minutes.
2. **Add Ingredients:** Add chickpeas, diced tomatoes, spinach, cumin, salt, and pepper to the skillet. Stir well and let the stew simmer for 15 minutes, allowing the flavors to meld together.
3. **Serve:** Garnish the stew with fresh herbs like parsley or cilantro before serving. Serve hot with crusty bread or over rice.

NUTRITIONAL INFO (PER SERVING): Calories: 180 | Protein: 6g | Carbohydrates: 24g | Fats: 7g | Fiber: 6g | Sodium: 200mg

Baked Polenta with Olive Tapenade

Yield: 4 servings
Prep Time: 15 minutes | **Cook Time:** 25 minutes

INGREDIENTS:

For the Polenta:
- 1 cup polenta (cornmeal) (160 g)
- 4 cups water or vegetable broth (960 ml)
- 1 tbsp olive oil (15 ml)
- Salt to taste
- 1/4 cup grated Parmesan cheese (optional, 25 g)

For the Olive Tapenade:
- 1/2 cup Kalamata olives, pitted (75 g)
- 1 tbsp capers (15 g)
- 2 garlic cloves, minced (6g)
- 2 tbsp olive oil (30 ml)
- 1 tbsp lemon juice (15 ml)
- Salt and pepper to taste
- Fresh parsley for garnish (optional, 5 g)

INSTRUCTIONS:

1. **Prepare the Polenta:** Bring water or broth to a boil. Whisk in polenta and cook for 15-20 minutes. Stir in salt and Parmesan, then spread the polenta onto a greased sheet to cool and firm up.
2. **Bake the Polenta:** Preheat oven to 400°F (200°C). Slice the firm polenta into squares brush with olive oil, and bake for 20-25 minutes.
3. **Make Tapenade:** Blend olives, capers, garlic, olive oil, and lemon juice in a food processor.
4. **Serve:** Serve polenta with tapenade and parsley.

NUTRITIONAL INFO (PER SERVING): Calories: 230 | Protein: 4g | Carbohydrates: 30g | Fats: 10g | Fiber: 3g | Sodium: 400mg

CHAPTER 7: VEGETARIAN MAINS

Vegetable Moussaka

Yield: 6 servings
Prep Time: 20 minutes | **Cook Time:** 40 minutes

INGREDIENTS:

- 2 eggplants, sliced (500 g)
- 2 zucchinis, sliced (300 g)
- 2 potatoes, sliced (400 g)
- 1 cup tomato sauce (240 ml)
- 1 cup béchamel sauce (240 ml)
- 2 tbsp olive oil (30 ml)
- Salt, pepper to taste
- Optional: Oregano, thyme (to taste)

INSTRUCTIONS:

1. **Prepare Vegetables:** Preheat oven to 375°F (190°C). Slice the eggplants, zucchinis, and potatoes. Season with salt and pepper.
2. **Roast Vegetables:** Place the sliced vegetables on a baking sheet, drizzle with olive oil, and roast for 20 minutes until tender.
3. **Layer Moussaka:** In a baking dish, layer the roasted vegetables, tomato sauce, and béchamel sauce.
4. **Bake:** Bake for 20 minutes until the top is bubbly and golden.

NUTRITIONAL INFO (PER SERVING): Calories: 250 | Protein: 5g | Carbohydrates: 28g | Fat: 13g | Fiber: 6g | Sodium: 300mg

Greek Spanakopita

Yield: 8 servings
Prep Time: 15 minutes | **Cook Time:** 30 minutes

INGREDIENTS:

- 1 lb spinach, chopped (450 g)
- 1 cup feta cheese, crumbled (150 g)
- 1 small onion, finely chopped (100 g)
- 1/4 cup fresh dill, chopped (15g)
- 2 eggs, beaten (100 g)
- 1/2 tsp salt (3 g)
- 1/4 tsp black pepper (1g)
- 10 sheets phyllo dough (250 g)
- 1/4 cup olive oil (60 ml)

INSTRUCTIONS:

1. **Prepare Filling:** In a bowl, mix spinach, feta cheese, onion, dill, eggs, salt, and pepper.
2. **Layer Phyllo:** Preheat the oven to 375°F (190°C). Brush a baking dish with olive oil. Layer 5 sheets of phyllo dough in the dish, brushing each sheet with olive oil.
3. **Add Filling:** Spread the spinach mixture evenly over the phyllo layers. Layer the remaining 5 sheets of phyllo on top, brushing each sheet with olive oil.
4. **Bake:** Bake for 30 minutes.

NUTRITIONAL INFO (PER SERVING): Calories: 200 | Protein: 7g | Carbohydrates: 18g | Fat: 12g | Fiber: 2g | Sodium: 350mg

Mediterranean Stuffed Eggplant

Yield: 4 servings
Prep Time: 15 minutes | **Cook Time:** 30 minutes

INGREDIENTS:

- 2 medium eggplants, halved (600 g)
- 1 cup tomatoes, diced (150 g)
- 1 onion, chopped (150 g)
- 2 cloves garlic, minced (6 g)
- 1 bell pepper, diced (120 g)
- 1/2 cup feta cheese, crumbled (75 g)
- 2 tbsp olive oil (30 ml)
- Salt, pepper to taste
- Optional: Parsley, oregano

INSTRUCTIONS:

1. **Prepare Eggplant:** Preheat the oven to 375°F (190°C). Scoop out the flesh of the eggplants, chop it, and set aside.
2. **Cook Filling:** In a skillet, sauté the onion, garlic, bell pepper, and chopped eggplant flesh in olive oil over medium heat for about 5 minutes, or until tender. Add diced tomatoes, salt, pepper, and optional herbs. Cook for an additional 5 minutes.
3. **Stuff and Bake:** Fill the eggplant halves with the cooked mixture and top with crumbled feta cheese. Place the stuffed eggplants in a baking dish and drizzle with olive oil. Bake for 30 minutes, or until the tops are golden.

NUTRITIONAL INFO (PER SERVING): Calories: 180 | Protein: 5g | Carbohydrates: 15g | Fat: 12g | Fiber: 6g | Sodium: 320mg

Falafel with Tzatziki Sauce

Yield: 4 servings
Prep Time: 20 minutes | **Cook Time:** 15 minutes

INGREDIENTS:

Falafel:
- 1 1/2 cups chickpeas, soaked (240 g)
- 1/2 onion, chopped (75 g)
- 2 cloves garlic (6 g)
- 1/4 cup parsley, chopped (15 g)
- 1 tsp cumin (2 g)
- 1 tsp coriander (2 g)
- 2 tbsp flour (15 g)
- Salt, pepper to taste

- Oil for frying

Tzatziki Sauce:
- 1 cup Greek yogurt (240 g)
- 1/2 cucumber, grated (75 g)
- 1 clove garlic, minced (3 g)
- 1 tbsp lemon juice (15 ml)
- 1 tbsp fresh dill, chopped (3g)
- Salt, pepper to taste

INSTRUCTIONS:

1. **Make Falafel Mix:** Blend chickpeas, onion, garlic, parsley, cumin, coriander, salt, and pepper in a food processor. Mix in flour. Shape the mixture into small balls or patties.
2. **Fry Falafel:** Heat oil in a skillet over medium heat. Fry the falafel in batches for about 3 minutes.
3. **Prepare Tzatziki:** Mix the Greek yogurt, grated cucumber, garlic, lemon juice, dill, salt, and pepper.
4. **Serve:** Plate the falafel with a side of tzatziki sauce and garnish with additional dill if desired.

NUTRITIONAL INFO (PER SERVING): Calories: 250 | Protein: 9g | Carbohydrates: 27g | Fat: 12g | Fiber: 7g | Sodium: 280mg

Mushroom and Spinach Stuffed Crepes

Yield: 4 servings
Prep Time: 15 minutes | **Cook Time:** 20 minutes

INGREDIENTS:

Crepes:
- 1 cup all-purpose flour (125 g)
- 2 eggs (100 g)
- 1/2 cup milk (120 ml)
- 1/2 cup water (120 ml)
- 1/4 tsp salt (1.5 g)
- 2 tbsp olive oil (30 ml)

Filling:
- 1 tbsp olive oil (15 ml)
- 1 cup mushrooms, sliced (100g)
- 2 cups spinach, chopped (60g)
- 1 clove garlic, minced (3 g)
- 1/4 cup feta cheese, crumbled (30 g)
- Salt, pepper to taste

INSTRUCTIONS:

1. **Prepare Crepe Batter:** Mix flour, eggs, milk, water, salt, and olive oil. Let it rest for 10 minutes.
2. **Cook Crepes:** Heat a non-stick skillet over medium heat. Pour 1/4 cup of the batter into the skillet and tilt to spread evenly. Cook each crepe for about 2 minutes per side until lightly golden.
3. **Make Filling:** In a separate pan, heat olive oil and sauté mushrooms and minced garlic. Add spinach and cook until wilted. Stir in crumbled feta cheese and season with salt and pepper.
4. **Assemble Crepes:** Spoon the filling onto each crepe, fold or roll them, and serve warm.

NUTRITIONAL INFO (PER SERVING): Calories: 220 | Protein: 8g | Carbohydrates: 20g | Fat: 12g | Fiber: 2g | Sodium: 250mg

Greek Vegetable and Feta Pie

Yield: 6 servings
Prep Time: 25 minutes | **Cook Time:** 45 minutes

INGREDIENTS:

- 1 sheet puff pastry (275 g)
- 2 tbsp olive oil (30 ml)
- 1 medium onion, diced (150 g)
- 2 cloves garlic, minced (6 g)
- 1 medium zucchini, diced (150 g)
- 1 red bell pepper, diced (120 g)
- 1 cup spinach, chopped (30 g)
- 1/2 cup feta cheese, crumbled (75 g)
- 1/4 cup fresh parsley, chopped (15 g)
- 1/2 tsp dried oregano (1g)
- Salt and pepper, to taste
- 1 egg, beaten (50 g)

INSTRUCTIONS:

1. **Preheat Oven:** Preheat oven to 375°F (190°C).
2. **Sauté Vegetables:** Heat olive oil in a skillet over medium. Sauté onion and garlic for 3 minutes. Add zucchini and bell pepper; cook for 5 more minutes. Stir in spinach until wilted. Season with oregano, salt, and pepper.
3. **Prepare Filling:** Remove from heat, mix in feta and parsley. Let cool slightly.
4. **Assemble Pie:** Roll out puff pastry, place in pie dish, and add filling. Fold excess pastry over filling.
5. **Bake:** Brush with beaten egg and bake for 30-35 minutes. Cool slightly before serving.

NUTRITIONAL INFO (PER SERVING): Calories: 250 | Protein: 7g | Carbohydrates: 22g | Fats: 16g | Fiber: 3g | Sodium: 320mg

Cauliflower Steak with Herb Sauce

Yield: 4 servings
Prep Time: 10 minutes | **Cook Time:** 25 minutes

INGREDIENTS:

- 2 large cauliflower heads, sliced into 1-inch steaks (800 g)
- 3 tbsp olive oil (45 ml)
- 1 tsp garlic powder (3 g)
- 1/4 cup fresh parsley, chopped (15 g)
- Salt and pepper, to taste
- 1/4 cup fresh cilantro, chopped (15 g)
- 2 tbsp lemon juice (30 ml)
- 1 tbsp capers (10 g)
- Optional: Red pepper flakes for heat

INSTRUCTIONS:

1. **Preheat Oven:** Set oven to 400°F (200°C).
2. **Prepare Cauliflower:** Brush the cauliflower steaks with 2 tbsp olive oil, and season with garlic powder, salt, and pepper.
3. **Roast:** Place the steaks on a baking sheet and roast for 20-25 minutes or until golden brown and tender, flipping halfway through.
4. **Make Herb Sauce:** In a food processor, blend parsley, cilantro, lemon juice, capers, and 1 tbsp olive oil. Adjust seasoning to taste.
5. **Serve:** Drizzle the herb sauce over the roasted cauliflower steaks and garnish with red pepper flakes, if desired.

NUTRITIONAL INFO (PER SERVING): Calories: 120 | Protein: 3g | Carbohydrates: 8g | Fats: 9g | Fiber: 3g | Sodium: 250mg

Couscous with Roasted Vegetables and Feta

Yield: 4 servings
Prep Time: 15 minutes | **Cook Time:** 30 minutes

INGREDIENTS:

- 1 cup couscous (180 g)
- 1 1/4 cups vegetable broth (300 ml)
- 1 red bell pepper, chopped (120 g)
- 1 zucchini, sliced (150 g)
- 1 eggplant, cubed (200g)
- 1 cup cherry tomatoes, halved (150 g)
- 2 tbsp olive oil (30 ml)
- 1/2 cup feta cheese, crumbled (75 g)
- Salt and pepper, to taste
- Optional herbs: parsley, mint (10 g each)

INSTRUCTIONS:

1. **Preheat oven:** Set to 400°F (200°C). Toss bell pepper, zucchini, eggplant, and cherry tomatoes with olive oil, salt, and pepper. Spread on a baking sheet.
2. **Roast vegetables:** Bake for 25-30 minutes until tender and slightly charred.
3. **Prepare couscous:** In a pot, bring vegetable broth to a boil. Add couscous, cover, and remove from heat. Let sit for 5 minutes.
4. **Combine:** Mix couscous with roasted vegetables in a bowl. Top with crumbled feta and fresh herbs.
5. **Serve:** Serve warm, garnished with a lemon wedge.

NUTRITIONAL INFO (PER SERVING): Calories: 240 | Protein: 6g | Carbohydrates: 28g | Fats: 12g | Fiber: 4g | Sodium: 320mg

Sweet Potato and Chickpea Curry

Yield: 4 servings
Prep Time: 15 minutes | **Cook Time:** 30 minutes

INGREDIENTS:

- 2 medium sweet potatoes, peeled and cubed (400 g)
- 1 can chickpeas, drained and rinsed (400 g)
- 1 can diced tomatoes (400 g)
- 1 cup spinach, chopped (30 g)
- 1 onion, finely chopped (150 g)
- 2 garlic cloves, minced (6 g)
- 1 tbsp olive oil (15 ml)
- 1 tbsp curry powder (8g)
- 1 tsp cumin (3 g)
- 1 tsp turmeric (3 g)
- 1/2 tsp paprika (1 g)
- Salt and pepper to taste
- Fresh cilantro, chopped (optional, 10 g)

INSTRUCTIONS:

1. **Heat** olive oil in a large skillet over medium heat. Add onion and garlic; sauté until soft.
2. **Stir** in curry powder, cumin, turmeric, and paprika. Cook for 1 minute until fragrant.
3. **Add** sweet potatoes, chickpeas, and tomatoes. Stir well. Cover and simmer for 20-25 minutes, until sweet potatoes are tender.
4. **Stir** in spinach. Cook until wilted. Season with salt and pepper.
5. **Garnish** with fresh cilantro if desired. Serve warm with a side of flatbread or rice.

NUTRITIONAL INFO (PER SERVING): Calories: 210 | Protein: 6g | Carbohydrates: 38g | Fats: 5g | Fiber: 8g | Sodium: 350mg

Mediterranean Quinoa Stuffed Peppers

Yield: 4 servings
Prep Time: 15 minutes | **Cook Time:** 30 minutes

INGREDIENTS:

- 4 large bell peppers, halved and seeds removed (500 g)
- 1 cup quinoa, rinsed (180 g)
- 2 cups vegetable broth (480 ml)
- 1 cup cherry tomatoes, halved (150 g)
- 1/2 cup feta cheese, crumbled (75 g)
- 1/4 cup Kalamata olives, sliced (35 g)
- 1/4 cup red onion, finely chopped (40 g)
- 2 tbsp olive oil (30 ml)
- 2 garlic cloves, minced (6g)
- 1 tsp dried oregano (1 g)
- Salt and pepper to taste
- Fresh parsley for garnish (optional, 5 g)

INSTRUCTIONS:

1. **Preheat oven** to 375°F (190°C).
2. **Cook** quinoa in vegetable broth until fluffy, about 15 minutes.
3. **In a skillet,** heat olive oil and sauté garlic until fragrant. Add cherry tomatoes, olives, and red onion. Cook for 5 minutes.
4. **Stir** in quinoa, feta, oregano, salt, and pepper.
5. **Fill** each bell pepper half with the quinoa.
6. **Place** stuffed peppers in a baking dish, cover with foil, and bake for 25-30 minutes.
7. **Garnish** with fresh parsley and serve warm.

NUTRITIONAL INFO (PER SERVING): Calories: 250 | Protein: 8g | Carbohydrates: 30g | Fats: 10g | Fiber: 5g | Sodium: 450mg

Roasted Butternut Squash and Lentil Salad

Yield: 4 servings
Prep Time: 15 minutes | **Cook Time:** 30 minutes

INGREDIENTS:

- 1 medium butternut squash, peeled and cubed (450 g)
- 1 cup green lentils, cooked (180 g)
- 2 cups mixed greens (60 g)
- 1 cup cherry tomatoes, halved (150 g)
- 1/2 red onion, thinly sliced (40 g)
- 1/4 cup crumbled feta cheese (35 g)
- 2 tbsp olive oil, divided (30 ml)
- 1 tbsp balsamic vinegar (15 ml)
- Salt and pepper, to taste
- Optional: Fresh herbs, such as parsley or thyme (5 g)

INSTRUCTIONS:

1. **Roast Squash:** Preheat oven to 400°F (200°C). Toss the butternut squash with 1 tbsp olive oil, salt, and pepper. Spread on a baking sheet and roast for 25-30 minutes until tender.
2. **Prepare Salad:** In a large bowl, combine cooked lentils, mixed greens, tomatoes, and red onion.
3. **Dress Salad:** Drizzle with the remaining olive oil and balsamic vinegar. Season with salt and pepper, and toss gently to coat.
4. **Assemble Dish:** Add the roasted squash to the salad. Top with crumbled feta and fresh herbs.
5. **Serve:** Serve immediately or chill.

NUTRITIONAL INFO (PER SERVING): Calories: 250 | Protein: 8g | Carbohydrates: 34g | Fats: 10g | Fiber: 9g | Sodium: 250mg

Sweet Potato and Feta Frittata

Yield: 4 servings
Prep Time: 15 minutes | **Cook Time:** 20 minutes

INGREDIENTS:

- 1 large sweet potato, peeled and thinly sliced (200 g)
- 6 large eggs
- 1/2 cup crumbled feta cheese (75 g)
- 2 tbsp olive oil (30 ml)
- 1/4 cup chopped fresh parsley (15 g)
- 1/4 cup chopped fresh chives (15 g)
- Salt and pepper, to taste

INSTRUCTIONS:

1. **Preheat oven** to 375°F (190°C).
2. **Heat** olive oil in an oven-safe skillet over medium heat. Add sweet potato slices and cook until tender, about 8 minutes.
3. **Whisk** eggs in a bowl, season with salt and pepper. Pour over the sweet potatoes in the skillet.
4. **Sprinkle** feta cheese, parsley, and chives on top. Cook on the stovetop for 5 minutes until edges begin to set.
5. **Transfer** skillet to the oven and bake for 10 minutes, or until eggs are fully set.
6. **Slice and serve** with a side of mixed greens.

NUTRITIONAL INFO (PER SERVING): Calories: 210 | Protein: 12g | Carbohydrates: 18g | Fats: 12g | Fiber: 3g | Sodium: 340mg

CHAPTER 8: SNACKS AND APPETIZERS

Hummus with Pita Chips

Yield: 4 servings
Prep Time: 10 minutes | **Cook Time:** 10 minutes

INGREDIENTS:

- 1 can (15 oz) chickpeas, drained and rinsed (425 g)
- 1/4 cup tahini (60 g)
- 2 tbsp olive oil, plus extra for drizzling (30 ml)
- 2 tbsp lemon juice (30 ml)
- 1 clove garlic, minced
- 1/2 tsp ground cumin (1 g)
- Salt, to taste
- Paprika, for garnish
- 4 pita bread, cut into wedges
- 1 tbsp olive oil (for pita chips) (15 ml)

INSTRUCTIONS:

1. **Prepare Hummus:** In a food processor, combine chickpeas, tahini, olive oil, lemon juice, garlic, cumin, and salt. Blend until smooth.
2. **Garnish:** Transfer hummus to a serving bowl. Drizzle with extra olive oil and sprinkle with paprika.
3. **Make Pita Chips:** Preheat oven to 375°F (190°C). Brush pita wedges with olive oil and arrange on a baking sheet. Bake for 10 minutes.
4. **Serve:** Serve hummus with warm pita chips.

NUTRITIONAL INFO (PER SERVING): Calories: 280 | Protein: 6g | Carbohydrates: 28g | Fats: 14g | Fiber: 6g | Sodium: 250mg

Greek Tzatziki with Fresh Vegetables

Yield: 4 servings
Prep Time: 10 minutes | **Cook Time:** 0 minutes

INGREDIENTS:

- 1 cup Greek yogurt (245 g)
- 1 cucumber, grated (120 g)
- 2 cloves garlic, minced
- 1 tbsp olive oil (15 ml)
- 1 tbsp fresh dill, chopped (5 g)
- 1 tbsp lemon juice (15 ml)
- Salt and pepper, to taste
- Fresh vegetables (cucumber slices, cherry tomatoes, carrot sticks, bell pepper strips)

INSTRUCTIONS:

1. **In a bowl,** mix Greek yogurt, grated cucumber, minced garlic, olive oil, dill, and lemon juice.
2. **Season** with salt and pepper. Stir until well combined.
3. **Serve** chilled with fresh vegetables on the side.

NUTRITIONAL INFO (PER SERVING): Calories: 120 | Protein: 6g | Carbohydrates: 10g | Fats: 6g | Fiber: 2g | Sodium: 100mg

Spanakopita Triangles

Yield: 4 servings
Prep Time: 20 minutes | **Cook Time:** 25 minutes

INGREDIENTS:

- 1 cup spinach, chopped (30 g)
- 1/2 cup feta cheese, crumbled (60 g)
- 1/4 cup onion, finely diced (40 g)
- 1 tbsp olive oil (15 ml)
- 1/4 tsp nutmeg
- 1/4 tsp black pepper
- 8 sheets phyllo dough
- 1/4 cup melted butter or olive oil, for brushing (60 ml)

INSTRUCTIONS:

1. **Prepare Filling:** In a skillet, heat olive oil over medium heat. Sauté onions until soft. Add spinach and cook until wilted. Remove from heat and mix in feta, nutmeg, and pepper.
2. **Prepare Phyllo Dough:** Lay one sheet of phyllo dough on a flat surface and brush with melted butter. Place another sheet on top and repeat.
3. **Form Triangles:** Cut phyllo sheets into strips. Place a spoonful of filling at one end of each strip. Fold into a triangle, like folding a flag, and continue until the end of the strip. Repeat with remaining strips and filling.
4. **Bake:** Place triangles on a baking sheet. Brush with more butter. Bake at 350°F (175°C) for 20-25 minutes, or until golden and crispy.

NUTRITIONAL INFO (PER SERVING): Calories: 210 | Protein: 6g | Carbohydrates: 12g | Fats: 15g | Fiber: 2g | Sodium: 340mg

Marinated Olives with Herbs

Yield: 4 servings
Prep Time: 10 minutes | **Cook Time:** 0 minutes

INGREDIENTS:

- 1 cup mixed green and black olives (150 g)
- 2 tbsp extra virgin olive oil (30 ml)
- 2 cloves garlic, thinly sliced
- 1 tbsp fresh rosemary, chopped (3 g)
- 1 tbsp fresh thyme leaves (2 g)
- 1 tsp lemon zest (2 g)
- 1/2 tsp crushed red pepper flakes (optional, 1 g)
- Salt and pepper to taste

INSTRUCTIONS:

1. **In a bowl,** combine olives, olive oil, garlic, rosemary, thyme, lemon zest, and red pepper flakes (if using).
2. **Season** with salt and pepper to taste. Mix well to coat the olives evenly.
3. **Let** the olives marinate for at least 30 minutes at room temperature to absorb flavors.
4. **Serve** in a bowl, drizzled with additional olive oil if desired.

NUTRITIONAL INFO (PER SERVING): Calories: 110 | Protein: 1g | Carbohydrates: 2g | Fats: 11g | Fiber: 1g | Sodium: 310mg

Baked Feta with Tomatoes and Oregano

Yield: 4 servings
Prep Time: 10 minutes | **Cook Time:** 20 minutes

INGREDIENTS:

- 7 oz feta cheese, block (200g)
- 2 cups cherry tomatoes, halved (300g)
- 2 tbsp olive oil (30ml)
- 1 tsp dried oregano (1g)
- 1 garlic clove, minced (3g)
- Salt and pepper, to taste
- Fresh basil leaves, for garnish (optional)

INSTRUCTIONS:

1. **Preheat Oven:** Heat oven to 375°F (190°C).
2. **Prepare Ingredients:** Place feta in a small baking dish and scatter cherry tomatoes around it.
3. **Season:** Drizzle olive oil over feta and tomatoes, and sprinkle with oregano, garlic, salt, and pepper.
4. **Bake:** Bake for 20 minutes, or until tomatoes are softened and feta is lightly browned.
5. **Serve:** Garnish with fresh basil if desired. Serve warm with crusty bread or pita.

NUTRITIONAL INFO (PER SERVING): Calories: 210 | Fat: 18g | Carbohydrates: 4g | Protein: 7g | Fiber: 1g | Sodium: 420mg

Falafel Balls with Tahini Sauce

Yield: 4 servings
Prep Time: 15 minutes | **Cook Time:** 20 minutes

INGREDIENTS:

Falafel Balls:
- 1 can (15 oz) chickpeas, drained and rinsed (425g)
- 1 small onion, chopped (50g)
- 2 cloves garlic, minced (6g)
- 1/4 cup fresh parsley, chopped (15g)
- 1 tsp ground cumin (2g)
- 1 tsp ground coriander (2g)
- 1/2 tsp baking powder (2g)
- Salt and pepper, to taste
- 2-3 tbsp flour or chickpea flour (15-20g)
- Olive oil, for frying

Tahini Sauce:
- 1/4 cup tahini (60g)
- 2 tbsp lemon juice (30ml)
- 1 clove garlic, minced (3g)
- 2-3 tbsp water (30-45ml)
- Salt, to taste

INSTRUCTIONS:

1. **Falafel Balls:** Blend chickpeas, onion, garlic, parsley, cumin, coriander, baking powder, salt, and pepper in a food processor. Stir in flour to bind and shape into small balls.
2. **Heat** olive oil in a skillet and fry falafel until golden brown, about 4-5 minutes.
3. **Tahini Sauce:** Whisk together tahini, lemon juice, garlic, and water. Adjust water for desired consistency.
4. **Serve** falafel with the sauce.

NUTRITIONAL INFO (PER SERVING): Calories: 230 | Protein: 8g | Carbohydrates: 28g | Fats: 10g | Fiber: 6g | Sodium: 250mg

Grilled Shrimp Skewers

Yield: 4 servings
Prep Time: 15 minutes | **Cook Time:** 10 minutes

INGREDIENTS:

- 1 lb shrimp, peeled and deveined (450g)
- 2 tbsp olive oil (30ml)
- 2 cloves garlic, minced (6g)
- Juice of 1 lemon (30ml)
- 1 tsp paprika (2g)
- 1/2 tsp salt (3g)
- 1/4 tsp black pepper (1g)
- Fresh parsley, chopped, for garnish (optional)

INSTRUCTIONS:

1. Marinate Shrimp: In a bowl, mix olive oil, garlic, lemon juice, paprika, salt, and pepper. Add shrimp and toss to coat. Marinate for 10 minutes.

2. Prepare Skewers: Thread marinated shrimp onto skewers.

3. Grill: Preheat grill to medium-high. Grill shrimp skewers for 2-3 minutes per side until shrimp are pink and cooked through.

4. Serve: Garnish with chopped parsley and serve with lemon wedges.

NUTRITIONAL INFO (PER SERVING): Calories: 180 | Protein: 22g | Carbohydrates: 1g | Fat: 9g | Fiber: 0g | Sodium: 510mg

Stuffed Dates with Goat Cheese

Yield: 4 servings
Prep Time: 10 minutes | **Cook Time:** None

INGREDIENTS:

- 12 large Medjool dates, pitted (200g)
- 1/2 cup goat cheese, softened (120g)
- 1 tbsp fresh rosemary, chopped (2g)
- 1 tbsp honey, optional (15ml)
- 2 tbsp chopped walnuts or almonds, optional (15g)

INSTRUCTIONS:

1. Prepare Dates: Slice each date lengthwise to remove the pits, creating an opening for the filling.

2. Stuff with Cheese: Fill each date with a small spoonful of softened goat cheese, pressing gently to secure the filling.

3. Add Herbs and Toppings: Sprinkle chopped rosemary over the stuffed dates. For added sweetness, drizzle with honey.

4. Finish with Nuts: Garnish with chopped walnuts or almonds for a bit of crunch, if desired.

5. Serve: Arrange on a serving platter and enjoy immediately or chill for later.

NUTRITIONAL INFO (PER SERVING): Calories: 140 | Protein: 3g | Carbohydrates: 23g | Fat: 5g | Fiber: 3g | Sodium: 80mg

Lemon and Herb Marinated Mozzarella

Yield: 4 servings
Prep Time: 10 minutes | **Cook Time:** 0 minutes

INGREDIENTS:

- 7 oz mozzarella balls (200g)
- 3 tbsp olive oil (45ml)
- Zest of 1 lemon
- 1 tbsp lemon juice (15ml)
- 1 tsp fresh basil, chopped (1g)
- 1 tsp fresh oregano, chopped (1g)
- 1/4 tsp red pepper flakes, optional (0.5g)
- Salt and pepper to taste

INSTRUCTIONS:

1. Prepare Marinade: In a medium bowl, combine olive oil, lemon zest, lemon juice, basil, oregano, red pepper flakes (if using), salt, and pepper. Whisk until well blended.

2. Marinate Mozzarella: Add mozzarella balls to the bowl. Gently toss to coat each piece with the lemon and herb mixture.

3. Rest and Serve: Allow mozzarella to marinate for 10 minutes at room temperature. Serve as an appetizer or salad topping.

NUTRITIONAL INFO (PER SERVING): Calories: 150 | Protein: 8g | Carbohydrates: 1g | Fat: 12g | Fiber: 0g | Sodium: 220mg

Spinach and Feta Phyllo Cups

Yield: 6 servings
Prep Time: 15 minutes | **Cook Time:** 20 minutes

INGREDIENTS:

- 12 sheets phyllo dough (340g)
- 2 cups fresh spinach, chopped (60g)
- 1 cup feta cheese, crumbled (150g)
- 2 tbsp olive oil (30ml)
- 1 garlic clove, minced (3g)
- Salt and pepper to taste
- Fresh dill or parsley, optional for garnish

INSTRUCTIONS:

1. Preheat Oven: Preheat oven to 375°F (190°C).

2. Prepare Phyllo Cups: Cut phyllo sheets into squares, layer them in a muffin tin, brushing with olive oil between layers.

3. Cook Spinach Filling: Sauté garlic in a skillet with olive oil until fragrant. Add spinach, cook until wilted, then mix in feta, seasoning with salt and pepper.

4. Assemble: Spoon spinach mixture into the phyllo cups.

5. Bake: Bake for 15-20 minutes until phyllo is golden and crispy.

6. Serve: Garnish with fresh dill or parsley if desired, and serve warm.

NUTRITIONAL INFO (PER SERVING): Calories: 180 | Protein: 5g | Carbohydrates: 12g | Fat: 12g | Fiber: 2g | Sodium: 250mg

Roasted Almonds with Sea Salt

Yield: 4 servings
Prep Time: 5 minutes | **Cook Time:** 15 minutes

INGREDIENTS:

- 2 cups raw almonds (280g)
- 1 tbsp olive oil (15ml)
- 1 tsp sea salt (5g), adjust to taste
- Optional: 1 tsp smoked paprika or rosemary (5g)

INSTRUCTIONS:

1. Preheat Oven: Set oven to 350°F (175°C) and let it preheat.
2. Prepare Almonds: In a large bowl, toss almonds with olive oil until coated. Sprinkle with sea salt and, if desired, smoked paprika or chopped rosemary.
3. Roast Almonds: Spread almonds on a baking sheet in a single layer. Roast for 12-15 minutes, stirring once or twice to ensure even roasting. Almonds should turn golden brown and fragrant.
4. Cool and Serve: Remove from oven and let cool on the baking sheet to crisp up. Serve as a snack or garnish.

NUTRITIONAL INFO (PER SERVING): Calories: 170 | Protein: 6g | Carbohydrates: 6g | Fat: 15g | Fiber: 3g | Sodium: 150mg

Chickpea and Herb Patties

Yield: 4 servings
Prep Time: 15 minutes | **Cook Time:** 15 minutes

INGREDIENTS:

- 1 can chickpeas, drained and rinsed (425g)
- 1/4 cup fresh parsley and cilantro, chopped (10g each)
- 1/2 small onion, finely chopped (30g)
- 2 cloves garlic, minced (6g)
- 1/2 tsp ground coriander (2g)
- 1 tsp ground cumin (5g)
- 1/4 tsp red pepper flakes (1g, optional)
- 1 egg (50g)
- 1/4 cup breadcrumbs (30g)
- Salt and pepper to taste
- 2 tbsp olive oil (30ml)

INSTRUCTIONS:

1. Blend: In a food processor, combine chickpeas, parsley, cilantro, onion, garlic, cumin, coriander, and red pepper flakes. Pulse until mixture is slightly chunky.
2. Mix: Transfer to a bowl. Add egg, breadcrumbs, salt, and pepper. Mix well to combine.
3. Shape Patties: Form mixture into 8 small patties.
4. Cook: Heat olive oil in a skillet over medium heat. Cook patties for 3-4 minutes on each side until golden brown and crisp.
5. Serve: Enjoy warm with a side salad or sauce.

NUTRITIONAL INFO (PER SERVING): Calories: 180 | Sugars: 3g | Fat: 8g | Carbohydrates: 22g | Protein: 6g | Fiber: 6g | Sodium: 240mg

CHAPTER 9: PASTA

Lemon and Herb Spaghetti

Yield: 4 servings
Prep Time: 10 minutes | **Cook Time:** 15 minutes

INGREDIENTS:

- 8 oz spaghetti (225g)
- 2 tbsp olive oil (30ml)
- 2 cloves garlic, minced (6g)
- 1 lemon, zested and juiced
- 1/4 cup fresh parsley, chopped (10g)
- 1/4 cup fresh basil, chopped (10g)
- Salt and pepper, to taste
- 1/4 cup grated Parmesan cheese (optional) (25g)
- Optional herbs/spices: red pepper flakes, thyme

INSTRUCTIONS:

1. Cook spaghetti: Boil water in a pot, add spaghetti, and cook until al dente (about 8-10 minutes). Drain.

2. Prepare sauce: In a skillet, heat olive oil over medium heat. Add garlic and sauté (1-2 minutes).

3. Combine: Add cooked spaghetti to the skillet. Toss with lemon juice, zest, parsley, and basil. Season with salt and pepper.

4. Serve: Transfer to plates and top with Parmesan cheese if desired. Garnish with additional herbs.

NUTRITIONAL INFO (PER SERVING): Calories: 250 | Fat: 8g | Carbohydrates: 40g | Protein: 7g | Fiber: 3g | Sodium: 150mg

Linguine with Clams and White Wine

Yield: 4 servings
Prep Time: 10 minutes | **Cook Time:** 20 minutes

INGREDIENTS:

- 12 oz linguine pasta (340g)
- 2 tbsp olive oil (30ml)
- 3 cloves garlic, minced (9g)
- 1/2 tsp red pepper flakes (optional)
- 1 cup dry white wine (240ml)
- 2 lbs fresh clams, scrubbed (900g)
- 1/4 cup fresh parsley, chopped (10g)
- Salt and pepper to taste
- Lemon wedges for serving

INSTRUCTIONS:

1. Cook linguine in salted water until al dente. Drain and set aside.

2. Heat olive oil in a large skillet. Add garlic and red pepper flakes; sauté for 1 minute.

3. Pour in white wine and bring to a simmer. Add clams, cover, and cook for 6-8 minutes, until clams open. Discard any unopened clams. Add linguine to skillet, tossing to coat with sauce.

4. Sprinkle with parsley, salt, and pepper.

NUTRITIONAL INFO (PER SERVING): Calories: 400 | Protein: 18g | Carbohydrates: 55g | Fat: 10g | Fiber: 2g | Sodium: 280mg

Spinach and Ricotta Ravioli with Sage Butter

Yield: 4 servings
Prep Time: 20 minutes | **Cook Time:** 15 minutes

INGREDIENTS:

For the Sage Butter:
- 4 tbsp butter (60g)
- 8 fresh sage leaves
- 2 tbsp grated Parmesan (10g)
- Salt and pepper to taste

For the Ravioli Dough and Filling:
- 1 3/4 cups whole grain flour (200g)
- 2 eggs
- 1 cup cooked spinach, chopped (150g)
- 3/4 cup ricotta (150g)
- 1/4 cup grated Parmesan (50g)
- Salt and pepper to taste

INSTRUCTIONS:

1. Make Dough: Mix flour, eggs, and a pinch of salt. Knead until smooth; rest 30 minutes.
2. Prepare Filling: Combine spinach, ricotta, Parmesan, salt, and pepper.
3. Assemble Ravioli: Roll out dough, add filling mounds, fold, and cut into squares. Seal edges.
4. Boil Ravioli: Cook in boiling water 3-4 minutes until floating.
5. Cook Sage Butter: Melt butter, add sage, cook until butter browns and sage crisps.
6. Serve: Toss ravioli in sage butter and top with Parmesan.

NUTRITIONAL INFO (PER SERVING): Calories: 290 | Protein: 10g | Carbohydrates: 32g | Fat: 6g | Fiber: 2g | Sodium: 320mg

Fettuccine Alfredo with Broccoli

Yield: 4 servings
Prep Time: 10 minutes | **Cook Time:** 20 minutes

INGREDIENTS:

- 8 oz fettuccine (225g)
- 2 cups broccoli florets (200g)
- 1 cup heavy cream (240ml)
- 1/2 cup grated Parmesan cheese (50g)
- 2 tbsp unsalted butter (30g)
- 2 cloves garlic, minced
- Salt and pepper to taste
- **Optional:** Red pepper flakes, fresh parsley

INSTRUCTIONS:

1. Cook Fettuccine: Boil fettuccine in salted water until al dente. Drain and set aside.
2. Steam Broccoli: In the last 3 minutes of pasta cooking, add broccoli florets to the pot. Drain with pasta.
3. Prepare Sauce: In a skillet, melt butter over medium heat. Sauté garlic until fragrant. Add cream and simmer for 3-4 minutes until slightly thickened.
4. Combine: Stir in Parmesan cheese. Add pasta and broccoli, tossing to coat. Season with salt, pepper, and optional red pepper flakes.
5. Serve: Garnish with fresh parsley and extra Parmesan if desired.

NUTRITIONAL INFO (PER SERVING): Calories: 400 | Protein: 12g | Carbohydrates: 50g | Fat: 18g | Fiber: 4g | Sodium: 300mg

Orzo with Lemon and Parmesan

Yield: 4 servings
Prep Time: 10 minutes | **Cook Time:** 15 minutes

INGREDIENTS:

- 1 cup orzo pasta (200g)
- 2 tbsp olive oil (30ml)
- 2 cloves garlic, minced
- 1 lemon, zested and juiced
- 1/2 cup grated Parmesan cheese (50g)
- Salt and pepper to taste
- Optional: Fresh parsley or basil for garnish

INSTRUCTIONS:

1. Cook orzo according to package instructions. Drain and set aside.
2. In a skillet, heat olive oil over medium heat. Add minced garlic and sauté until fragrant.
3. Stir in cooked orzo, lemon juice, and zest. Mix well.
4. Remove from heat, stir in Parmesan cheese. Season with salt and pepper.
5. Garnish with fresh herbs if desired. Serve warm.

NUTRITIONAL INFO (PER SERVING): Calories: 220 | Fat: 8g | Carbohydrates: 30g | Protein: 6g | Fiber: 2g | Sodium: 200mg

Shrimp Scampi with Angel Hair Pasta

Yield: 4 servings
Prep Time: 10 minutes | **Cook Time:** 15 minutes

INGREDIENTS:

- 8 oz angel hair pasta (225g)
- 1 lb shrimp, peeled and deveined (450g)
- 4 cloves garlic, minced
- 1/4 cup olive oil (60ml)
- 1/4 cup white wine (60ml)
- Juice of 1 lemon
- 1/4 cup fresh parsley, chopped (15g)
- Salt and pepper to taste
- Red pepper flakes (optional)

INSTRUCTIONS:

1. Cook pasta according to package directions. Drain and set aside.
2. In a skillet, heat olive oil over medium heat. Add garlic and sauté until fragrant.
3. Add shrimp and cook until pink, about 2-3 minutes per side.
4. Pour in white wine and lemon juice, simmer for 2 minutes.
5. Toss in cooked pasta, parsley, salt, pepper, and red pepper flakes.
6. Serve hot.

NUTRITIONAL INFO (PER SERVING): Calories: 410 | Fat: 12g | Carbohydrates: 45g | Protein: 28g | Fiber: 2g | Sodium: 620mg

Tagliatelle with Asparagus and Lemon

Yield: 4 servings
Prep Time: 10 minutes | **Cook Time:** 15 minutes

INGREDIENTS:

- 8 oz tagliatelle pasta (225g)
- 1 lb asparagus, trimmed and cut into 2-inch pieces (450g)
- 2 tbsp olive oil (30ml)
- 2 cloves garlic, minced
- Zest and juice of 1 lemon
- Salt and pepper to taste
- 1/4 cup grated Parmesan cheese (optional) (25g)
- Fresh parsley, chopped (optional)

INSTRUCTIONS:

1. **Cook** the tagliatelle according to package instructions. Drain and set aside.
2. **In a skillet,** heat olive oil over medium heat. Add garlic and sauté for 1 minute.
3. **Add** asparagus and cook for 5-7 minutes until tender.
4. **Add** cooked tagliatelle, lemon zest, lemon juice, salt, and pepper to the skillet. Toss to combine.
5. **Optional:** Top with grated Parmesan and fresh parsley before serving.

NUTRITIONAL INFO (PER SERVING): Calories: 320 | Protein: 10g | Carbohydrates: 50g | Fat: 10g | Fiber: 5g | Sodium: 150mg

Orzo Salad with Feta and Olives

Yield: 4 servings
Prep Time: 15 minutes | **Cook Time:** 10 minutes

INGREDIENTS:

- 1 cup orzo (200g)
- 1/2 cup crumbled feta cheese (75g)
- 1/2 cup pitted Kalamata olives, halved (75g)
- 1/2 cup cherry tomatoes, halved (75g)
- 1/4 cup chopped red onion (35g)
- 2 tbsp olive oil (30ml)
- 1 tbsp lemon juice (15ml)
- 1 tsp dried oregano (2g)
- Salt and pepper to taste
- Optional: chopped fresh parsley for garnish

INSTRUCTIONS:

1. **Cook** orzo according to package instructions. Drain and cool.
2. **In a large bowl,** combine orzo, feta, olives, tomatoes, and red onion.
3. **In a small bowl,** whisk together olive oil, lemon juice, oregano, salt, and pepper. Pour over salad and toss to coat.
4. **Garnish** with parsley, if desired. Serve chilled.

NUTRITIONAL INFO (PER SERVING): Calories: 250 | Protein: 6g | Carbohydrates: 30g | Fat: 12g | Fiber: 3g | Sodium: 500mg

Gnocchi with Sage and Brown Butter

Yield: 4 servings
Prep Time: 10 minutes | **Cook Time:** 15 minutes

INGREDIENTS:

- 1 lb potato gnocchi (450g)
- 4 tbsp unsalted butter (60g)
- 10 fresh sage leaves, chopped
- Salt and pepper to taste
- Grated Parmesan cheese (optional)

INSTRUCTIONS:

1. Cook Gnocchi: Bring a large pot of salted water to a boil. Add gnocchi and cook until they float to the surface, about 2-3 minutes. Drain and set aside.
2. Brown Butter: In a large skillet over medium heat, melt butter. Once melted, add sage leaves and cook, stirring occasionally, until butter turns golden brown and sage is crispy, about 3-4 minutes.
3. Combine: Add gnocchi to the skillet with browned butter and sage. Toss gently to coat. Season with salt and pepper to taste.
4. Serve: Plate and sprinkle with Parmesan cheese, if desired. Serve immediately.

NUTRITIONAL INFO (PER SERVING): Calories: 280 | Protein: 5g | Carbohydrates: 42g | Fat: 11g | Fiber: 2g | Sodium: 180mg

Baked Penne with Mozzarella and Tomatoes

Yield: 4 servings
Prep Time: 15 minutes | **Cook Time:** 25 minutes

INGREDIENTS:

- 8 oz penne pasta (225g)
- 1 ½ cups mozzarella, cubed (200g)
- 2 cups cherry tomatoes, halved (400g)
- 2 tbsp olive oil (30ml)
- 2 cloves garlic, minced
- 1 tsp dried oregano (2g)
- Salt and pepper to taste
- Fresh basil for garnish (optional)

INSTRUCTIONS:

1. Preheat oven to 375°F (190°C).
2. Cook penne according to package instructions. Drain and set aside.
3. In a skillet, heat olive oil over medium heat. Add garlic and sauté until fragrant.
4. Add tomatoes, oregano, salt, and pepper. Cook until tomatoes soften, about 5 minutes.
5. Combine cooked penne with tomato mixture and mozzarella in a baking dish, mixing well.
6. Bake for 20 minutes or until mozzarella is melted and bubbly.
7. Garnish with fresh basil, if desired. Serve hot.

NUTRITIONAL INFO (PER SERVING): Calories: 320 | Protein: 12g | Carbohydrates: 40g | Fat: 12g | Fiber: 4g | Sodium: 400mg

30-DAY MEAL PLAN

Day	Breakfast	Lunch	Snack	Dinner
Day 1	Mediterranean Shakshuka - p.9	Greek Salad with Feta and Olives - p.17	Marinated Olives with Herbs - p.56	Roasted Halibut with Mediterranean Vegetables - p.33
Day 2	Olive Oil and Lemon Pancakes - p.9	Lentil Salad with Fresh Mint and Feta - p.19	Hummus with Pita Chips - p.55	Spiced Meatballs with Tomato Sauce - p.28
Day 3	Feta and Spinach Omelet - p.10	Mixed Green Salad with Pear and Gorgonzola - p.21	Spanakopita Triangles - p.56	Grilled Rabbit with Garlic and Herbs - p.29
Day 4	Breakfast Couscous with Dried Fruits - p.10	Farro Salad with Roasted Red Peppers - p.22	Lemon and Herb Marinated Mozzarella - p.59	Herb-Crusted Baked Trout - p.35
Day 5	Overnight Oats with Almonds and Dates - p.11	Shrimp and Avocado Salad - p.23	Roasted Almonds with Sea Salt - p.60	Chicken Souvlaki with Garlic Sauce - p.27
Day 6	Warm Quinoa Porridge with Berries - p.11	Tuna Salad with White Beans - p.21	Chickpea and Herb Patties - p.60	Sardines with Lemon and Parsley - p.36
Day 7	Mediterranean Frittata - p.12	Roasted Sweet Potato and Feta Salad - p.26	Stuffed Dates with Goat Cheese - p.58	Mediterranean Stuffed Eggplant - p.50
Day 8	Greek Yogurt Parfait with Fresh Fruit - p.12	Grilled Halloumi and Vegetable Salad - p.24	Spinach and Feta Phyllo Cups - p.59	Rabbit with Wild Mushrooms and Garlic - p.31
Day 9	Hummus and Veggie Breakfast Wrap - p.13	Arugula Salad with Prosciutto and Melon - p.25	Marinated Grilled Vegetables - p.47	Baked Sea Bass with Tomatoes - p.37
Day 10	Spinach and Ricotta Stuffed Peppers - p.13	Roasted Vegetable and Arugula Salad - p.20	Falafel Balls with Tahini Sauce - p.57	Shrimp Skewers with Spicy Yogurt Sauce - p.39
Day 11	Fresh Fruit Salad with Citrus Dressing - p.14	Cucumber and Dill Salad with Yogurt Dressing - p.24	Greek Tzatziki with Fresh Vegetables - p.55	Tuna Steaks with Caper Relish - p.34
Day 12	Millet Porridge with Almond Milk - p.14	Grilled Chicken Caesar Salad - p.19	Grilled Shrimp Skewers - p.58	Vegetable Moussaka - p.49
Day 13	Breakfast Couscous Salad - p.15	Spinach Salad with Oranges and Almonds - p.20	Baked Feta with Tomatoes and Oregano - p.57	Mediterranean Baked Cod - p.33
Day 14	Baked Oatmeal with Apples and Cinnamon - p.15	Quinoa Tabbouleh with Fresh Herbs - p.17	Roasted Cauliflower with Tahini Sauce - p.44	Rabbit with Lemon and Oregano Marinade - p.30
Day 15	Mediterranean Smoothie Bowl - p.16	Tomato and Cucumber Salad with Red Onion - p.18	Stuffed Grape Leaves with Rice - p.44	Grilled Swordfish with Olive Tapenade - p.34
Day 16	Honey and Almond Granola - p.16	Lentil Pilaf with Caramelized Onions - p.45	Lemon and Herb Spaghetti - p.61	Mussels in White Wine Sauce - p.35

Day	Breakfast	Lunch	Snack	Dinner
Day 17	Mediterranean Shakshuka - p.9	Beet and Goat Cheese Salad - p.22	Marinated Olives with Herbs - p.56	Chicken Marbella with Olives and Capers - p.27
Day 18	Olive Oil and Lemon Pancakes - p.9	Grilled Salmon Salad with Lemon Dressing - p.26	Lemon and Herb Marinated Mozzarella - p.59	Stuffed Squid with Rice and Herbs - p.39
Day 19	Feta and Spinach Omelet - p.10	Carrot and Orange Salad with Walnuts - p.25	Hummus with Pita Chips - p.55	Saffron Shrimp Risotto - p.40
Day 20	Breakfast Couscous with Dried Fruits - p.10	Grilled Halloumi and Vegetable Salad - p.24	Spinach and Feta Phyllo Cups - p.59	Beef Moussaka - p.29
Day 21	Warm Quinoa Porridge with Berries - p.11	Arugula Salad with Prosciutto and Melon - p.25	Falafel Balls with Tahini Sauce - p.57	Herb-Crusted Baked Trout - p.35
Day 22	Mediterranean Frittata - p.12	Tomato and Cucumber Salad with Red Onion - p.18	Roasted Almonds with Sea Salt - p.60	Chicken with Artichokes and Olives - p.28
Day 23	Greek Yogurt Parfait with Fresh Fruit - p.12	Lentil Salad with Fresh Mint and Feta - p.19	Chickpea and Herb Patties - p.60	Baked Clams with Oregano and Lemon - p.40
Day 24	Hummus and Veggie Breakfast Wrap - p.13	Spinach Salad with Oranges and Almonds - p.20	Spanakopita Triangles - p.56	Roasted Halibut with Mediterranean Vegetables - p.33
Day 25	Spinach and Ricotta Stuffed Peppers - p.13	Quinoa Tabbouleh with Fresh Herbs - p.17	Greek Tzatziki with Fresh Vegetables - p.55	Sardines with Lemon and Parsley - p.36
Day 26	Fresh Fruit Salad with Citrus Dressing - p.14	Grilled Chicken Caesar Salad - p.19	Roasted Cauliflower with Tahini Sauce - p.44	Mediterranean Stuffed Eggplant - p.50
Day 27	Millet Porridge with Almond Milk - p.14	Beet and Goat Cheese Salad - p.22	Lemon and Herb Spaghetti - p.61	Tuna Tartare with Avocado - p.41
Day 28	Breakfast Couscous Salad - p.15	Mixed Green Salad with Pear and Gorgonzola - p.21	Marinated Grilled Vegetables - p.47	Shrimp Skewers with Spicy Yogurt Sauce - p.39
Day 29	Baked Oatmeal with Apples and Cinnamon - p.15	Tuna Salad with White Beans - p.21	Roasted Almonds with Sea Salt - p.60	Mediterranean Baked Cod - p.33
Day 30	Mediterranean Smoothie Bowl - p.16	Farro Salad with Roasted Red Peppers - p.22	Stuffed Dates with Goat Cheese - p.58	Chicken Marbella with Olives and Capers - p.27

Note: The 30-Day Meal Plan is designed as a flexible framework, offering a variety of wholesome meals with balanced proportions of proteins, healthy fats, and carbohydrates. Calorie estimates are provided as a guideline and may vary depending on ingredient choices and portion sizes. This plan encourages a nutritious and flavorful approach to eating while allowing room for customization to suit individual tastes and dietary needs. Feel free to adapt recipes and portion sizes to align with your personal preferences and lifestyle. Enjoy the journey to delicious and healthy Mediterranean-inspired meals!

BONUSES

Meal Planning and Shopping Templates

Welcome to your tailored 30-day grocery shopping guide, thoughtfully designed to accompany the flavorful Mediterranean recipes in this cookbook. Created with a focus on fresh, wholesome ingredients, this guide is perfect for individuals aiming to embrace the health benefits of the Mediterranean diet. Carefully portioned for one person, it ensures minimal waste while maximizing flavor and nutrition. By prioritizing fresh produce, whole grains, lean proteins, and heart-healthy fats, this guide supports balanced eating habits.

Shopping List for 7-Day Meal Plan

Meat & Poultry

- Ground beef (85% lean) – 1 lb / 450 g (Spiced Meatballs)
- Chicken breast – 1 lb / 450 g (Chicken Souvlaki)
- Rabbit (whole or cuts) – 1.5 lb / 680 g (Grilled Rabbit with Garlic and Herbs)

Fish & Seafood

- Halibut fillets – 8 oz / 225 g (Roasted Halibut)
- Trout fillets – 8 oz / 225 g (Herb-Crusted Trout)
- Shrimp (peeled and deveined) – 6 oz / 170 g (Shrimp and Avocado Salad)
- Sardines (fresh or canned) – 4 fillets (Sardines with Lemon and Parsley)

Vegetables

- Bell peppers (red and green) – 3 medium (Greek Salad, Mediterranean Stuffed Eggplant)
- Tomatoes – 12 medium (Shakshuka, Greek Salad, Lentil Salad, Eggplant)
- Cucumbers – 2 medium (Greek Salad, Tuna Salad)
- Zucchini – 3 medium (Stuffed Eggplant, Frittata)
- Eggplant – 2 large (Mediterranean Stuffed Eggplant)
- Sweet potato – 1 large (Sweet Potato Salad)
- Red onion – 2 medium (Greek Salad, Tuna Salad)
- Garlic – 1 bulb (Various recipes)
- Spinach (fresh) – 4 cups / 120 g (Frittata, Omelet, Lentil Salad)
- Mixed greens – 2 cups / 60 g (Mixed Green Salad)
- Fresh herbs (parsley, mint, dill) – 1 bunch each (Lentil Salad, Meatballs, Mozzarella)
- Kalamata olives – 1 small jar (Greek Salad, Marinated Olives)

Fruits

- Lemons – 6 medium (Various recipes)
- Berries (blueberries or mixed) – 1 pint / 300 g (Quinoa Porridge)
- Dried fruits (apricots, dates) – 1 cup / 150 g (Couscous, Overnight Oats)
- Pear – 1 medium (Mixed Green Salad)

Grains & Bread

- Quinoa – 1 cup / 180 g (Quinoa Porridge)
- Couscous – 1 cup / 180 g (Breakfast Couscous)
- Farro – 1 cup / 180 g (Farro Salad)
- Pita bread – 2 small (Hummus and Chips)

Dairy & Eggs

- Feta cheese – 12 oz / 340 g (Greek Salad, Sweet Potato Salad)
- Gorgonzola cheese – 2 oz / 60 g (Mixed Green Salad)
- Greek yogurt (plain, full-fat) – 2 cups / 500 g (Hummus, Mozzarella)
- Eggs – 18 large (Shakshuka, Omelet, Frittata, Pancakes)
- Mozzarella (fresh) – 8 oz / 225 g (Marinated Mozzarella)

Nuts, Seeds & Nut Butter

- Almonds (whole or chopped) – ½ cup / 75 g (Overnight Oats, Roasted Almonds)
- Walnuts (chopped) – ¼ cup / 40 g (Stuffed Dates)

Pantry Staples

- Olive oil (extra virgin) – 1 bottle (Various recipes)
- Tahini – 1 small jar (Hummus)
- Honey – 1 small jar (Pancakes, Sweet Potato Salad)
- Tomato paste – 1 small can (Shakshuka, Meatballs)
- Spices (paprika, cumin, oregano, cinnamon) – 1 small jar each

Shopping List for 8-14 Day Meal Plan

Meat & Poultry

- Rabbit (cuts or whole) – 2 lb / 900 g (Rabbit with Wild Mushrooms, Rabbit with Lemon Marinade)
- Chicken breast – 1 lb / 450 g (Grilled Chicken Caesar Salad)

Fish & Seafood

- Sea bass fillets – 8 oz / 225 g (Baked Sea Bass)
- Cod fillets – 12 oz / 340 g (Mediterranean Baked Cod)
- Shrimp (peeled and deveined) – 12 oz / 340 g (Grilled Shrimp Skewers, Shrimp Skewers with

Yogurt Sauce)
- Tuna steaks – 8 oz / 225 g (Tuna Steaks with Caper Relish)

Vegetables

- Bell peppers (red and yellow) – 3 medium (Stuffed Peppers, Grilled Vegetables)
- Cherry tomatoes – 3 cups / 450 g (Parfait, Baked Feta, Roasted Vegetables, Baked Sea Bass)
- Eggplant – 2 medium (Vegetable Moussaka, Grilled Vegetables)
- Zucchini – 3 medium (Grilled Vegetables, Moussaka, Quinoa Tabbouleh)
- Spinach (fresh) – 6 cups / 180 g (Stuffed Peppers, Spinach Salad, Grilled Vegetables)
- Mixed greens (arugula, lettuce) – 3 cups / 90 g (Grilled Halloumi Salad, Caesar Salad)
- Cucumber – 2 medium (Tzatziki, Cucumber Salad, Veggie Wrap)
- Red onion – 2 medium (Quinoa Tabbouleh, Grilled Vegetables)
- Garlic – 1 bulb (Various recipes)
- Fresh herbs (parsley, dill, mint, oregano) – 1 bunch each (Quinoa Tabbouleh, Tzatziki, Cucumber Salad)
- Mushrooms – 8 oz / 225 g (Rabbit with Mushrooms, Grilled Vegetables)
- Cauliflower – 1 small head (Roasted Cauliflower)
- Lemons – 6 medium (Citrus Dressing, Tzatziki, Caper Relish)

Fruits

- Apples – 2 medium (Baked Oatmeal)
- Oranges – 2 medium (Spinach Salad, Citrus Dressing)
- Melon (cantaloupe or honeydew) – ½ medium (Arugula Salad)
- Berries (mixed or strawberries) – 1 pint / 300 g (Parfait, Fruit Salad)
- Dates – ½ cup / 75 g (Parfait, Couscous Salad)

Grains & Bread

- Millet – ½ cup / 90 g (Millet Porridge)
- Quinoa – 1 cup / 180 g (Quinoa Tabbouleh)
- Couscous – 1 cup / 180 g (Breakfast Couscous Salad)
- Phyllo dough – 4 sheets (Phyllo Cups)
- Pita bread – 2 small (Hummus Wrap, Tzatziki)
- Oats (rolled) – 1 cup / 90 g (Baked Oatmeal)

Dairy & Eggs

- Feta cheese – 12 oz / 340 g (Grilled Halloumi Salad, Spinach Salad, Baked Feta)
- Halloumi cheese – 8 oz / 225 g (Grilled Halloumi Salad)
- Greek yogurt (plain, full-fat) – 3 cups / 750 g (Parfait, Tzatziki, Yogurt Sauce)
- Ricotta cheese – 8 oz / 225 g (Stuffed Peppers)
- Eggs – 10 large (Baked Oatmeal, Phyllo Cups, Moussaka)

Nuts, Seeds & Nut Butter

- Almonds (chopped) – ½ cup / 75 g (Spinach Salad, Millet Porridge)
- Tahini – ½ cup / 75 g (Falafel, Cauliflower, Tzatziki)

Pantry Staples

- Olive oil (extra virgin) – 1 bottle (Various recipes)
- Honey – 1 small jar (Parfait, Spinach Salad, Oatmeal)
- Capers – 2 tbsp / 30 g (Tuna Steaks)
- Spices (cinnamon, cumin, oregano, paprika) – 1 small jar each (Various recipes)

Shopping List for 15-21 Day Meal Plan

Meat & Poultry

- Chicken thighs (bone-in) – 1 lb / 450 g (Chicken Marbella)
- Ground beef or lamb – 1 lb / 450 g (Beef Moussaka)

Fish & Seafood

- Swordfish steaks – 8 oz / 225 g (Grilled Swordfish)
- Mussels – 1 lb / 450 g (Mussels in White Wine Sauce)
- Salmon fillets – 8 oz / 225 g (Grilled Salmon Salad)
- Squid (cleaned) – 10 oz / 280 g (Stuffed Squid)
- Shrimp (peeled and deveined) – 12 oz / 340 g (Saffron Shrimp Risotto)
- Trout fillets – 8 oz / 225 g (Herb-Crusted Baked Trout)

Vegetables

- Bell peppers (various colors) – 3 medium (Grilled Vegetables, Moussaka)
- Cherry tomatoes – 3 cups / 450 g (Salad, Shakshuka, Vegetable Salad)
- Tomatoes – 4 medium (Shakshuka, Salad)
- Cucumbers – 2 medium (Tomato and Cucumber Salad)
- Red onion – 3 medium (Salad, Pilaf)
- Yellow onion – 2 large (Pilaf, Moussaka)
- Beets (cooked or fresh) – 2 medium (Beet Salad)
- Spinach (fresh) – 6 cups / 180 g (Feta Omelet, Grilled Salad, Moussaka)
- Zucchini – 2 medium (Moussaka)
- Eggplant – 2 medium (Moussaka)
- Carrots – 2 medium (Carrot Salad)
- Lemons – 6 medium (Dressing, Tapenade, Risotto)
- Fresh herbs (parsley, dill, mint, oregano, basil) – 1 bunch each (Various recipes)
- Garlic – 1 bulb (Various recipes)
- Grapes leaves (jarred or fresh) – 12 leaves (Stuffed Grape Leaves)
- Arugula – 4 cups / 120 g (Grilled Salad, Melon Salad)

Fruits

- Oranges – 2 medium (Carrot Salad)
- Berries (mixed) – 1 pint / 300 g (Smoothie Bowl, Quinoa Porridge)
- Dried fruits (apricots, raisins, or dates) – ½ cup / 75 g (Breakfast Couscous)

Grains & Bread

- Rice (long-grain or basmati) – 1 cup / 180 g (Stuffed Grape Leaves, Stuffed Squid)
- Quinoa – ½ cup / 90 g (Warm Quinoa Porridge)
- Lentils – 1 cup / 180 g (Lentil Pilaf)
- Spaghetti (whole grain or regular) – 8 oz / 225 g (Lemon and Herb Spaghetti)
- Pita bread – 2 small (Hummus with Pita Chips)
- Phyllo dough – 4 sheets (Spinach and Feta Phyllo Cups)

Dairy & Eggs

- Feta cheese – 10 oz / 280 g (Omelet, Salad, Phyllo Cups)
- Goat cheese – 4 oz / 120 g (Beet Salad)
- Halloumi cheese – 8 oz / 225 g (Grilled Salad)
- Parmesan cheese (grated) – 6 oz / 170 g (Shrimp Risotto, Spaghetti)
- Greek yogurt (plain, full-fat) – 1 cup / 250 g (Smoothie Bowl)
- Eggs – 8 large (Omelet, Shakshuka, Phyllo Cups)

Nuts, Seeds & Nut Butter

- Almonds (chopped) – ½ cup / 75 g (Granola, Carrot Salad)
- Walnuts (chopped) – ½ cup / 75 g (Carrot Salad)
- Pine nuts – 2 tbsp / 30 g (Salads)

Pantry Staples

- Olive oil (extra virgin) – 1 bottle (Various recipes)
- Honey – 1 small jar (Granola, Salad Dressing)
- Capers – 2 tbsp / 30 g (Tapenade, Marbella)
- Tahini – ½ cup / 75 g (Falafel, Salad Dressing)
- Spices (paprika, cumin, cinnamon, saffron, nutmeg) – 1 jar each (Various recipes)

Shopping List for 22-28 Day Meal Plan

Meat & Poultry

- Chicken breast (boneless,

skinless) – 12 oz / 340 g (Chicken with Artichokes)
- Sardines (fresh or canned) – 8 oz / 225 g (Sardines with Lemon)
- Shrimp (peeled and deveined) – 10 oz / 280 g (Shrimp Skewers)

Fish & Seafood

- Halibut fillets – 8 oz / 225 g (Roasted Halibut)
- Clams (fresh) – 12 oz / 340 g (Baked Clams)
- Tuna (fresh, sushi-grade) – 8 oz / 225 g (Tuna Tartare)

Vegetables

- Spinach (fresh) – 8 cups / 240 g (Frittata, Salad, Stuffed Peppers)
- Tomatoes – 6 medium (Tomato Salad, Tabbouleh)
- Cherry tomatoes – 2 cups / 300 g (Frittata, Caesar Salad)
- Cucumber – 2 medium (Tomato Salad, Tzatziki)
- Red onion – 2 medium (Salads)
- Bell peppers (various colors) – 4 medium (Stuffed Peppers, Grilled Vegetables)
- Eggplant – 2 medium (Stuffed Eggplant)
- Zucchini – 2 medium (Grilled Vegetables)
- Carrots – 2 medium (Salads)
- Cauliflower – 1 small head (Tahini Cauliflower)
- Artichokes (jarred or fresh) – 2 medium (Chicken with Artichokes)
- Fresh herbs (parsley, mint, dill, oregano, basil) – 1 bunch each (Various recipes)
- Garlic – 1 bulb (Various recipes)
- Lemons – 6 medium (Salads, Tabbouleh, Clams, Sardines)
- Oranges – 2 medium (Spinach Salad)

Fruits

- Fresh berries (mixed) – 1 pint / 300 g (Parfait)
- Pear – 1 medium (Mixed Salad)
- Dried fruits (apricots, raisins, or dates) – ½ cup / 75 g (Breakfast Couscous)

Grains & Bread

- Quinoa – 1 cup / 180 g (Tabbouleh)
- Millet – ½ cup / 90 g (Millet Porridge)
- Couscous – ½ cup / 90 g (Breakfast Couscous Salad)
- Whole grain pita bread – 2 small (Breakfast Wrap)

Dairy & Eggs

- Feta cheese – 8 oz / 225 g (Salads, Stuffed Peppers)
- Gorgonzola cheese – 4 oz / 120 g (Mixed Salad)
- Greek yogurt (plain, full-fat) – 1 cup / 250 g (Parfait, Tzatziki)
- Ricotta cheese – 4 oz / 120 g (Stuffed Peppers)
- Goat cheese – 4 oz / 120 g (Beet Salad)
- Eggs – 8 large (Frittata, Spanakopita Triangles)

Nuts, Seeds & Nut Butter

- Almonds (whole or chopped) – ½ cup / 75 g (Spinach Salad)
- Walnuts (chopped) – ½ cup / 75 g (Beet Salad)

Pantry Staples

- Olive oil (extra virgin) – 1 bottle
- Tahini – ½ cup / 75 g (Cauliflower Sauce)
- Honey – 1 small jar (Dressing, Parfait)
- Capers – 2 tbsp / 30 g (Tuna Tartare)
- Spices (paprika, cumin, cinnamon, saffron, nutmeg) – 1 jar each (Various recipes)

APPENDIX MEASUREMENT CONVERSION CHART

VOLUME EQUIVALENTS (DRY)

US STANDARD	METRIC (APPROXIMATE)
1/8 teaspoon	0.5 mL
1/4 teaspoon	1 mL
1/2 teaspoon	2 mL
3/4 teaspoon	4 mL
1 teaspoon	5 mL
1 tablespoon	15 mL
1/4 cup	59 mL
1/2 cup	118 mL
3/4 cup	177 mL
1 cup	235 mL
2 cups	475 mL
3 cups	700 mL
4 cups	1 L

VOLUME EQUIVALENTS (LIQUID)

US STANDARD	US STANDARD (OUNCES)	METRIC (AP PROXIMATE)
2 tablespoons	1 fl.oz.	30 mL
1/4 cup	2 fl.oz.	60 mL
1/2 cup	4 fl.oz.	120 mL
1 cup	8 fl.oz.	240 mL
11/2 cup	12 fl.oz.	355 mL
2 cups or 1 pint	16 fl.oz.	475 mL
4 cups or 1 quart	32 fl.oz.	1 L
1 gallon	128 fl.oz.	4 L

WEIGHT EQUIVALENTS

US STANDARD	METRIC (APPROXIMATE)
1 ounce	28 g
2 ounces	57 g
5 ounces	142 g
10 ounces	284 g
15 ounces	425 g
16 ounces	455 g
(1 pound)	680 g
1.5 pounds	907 g

TEMPERATURES EQUIVALENTS

FAHRENHEIT(F)	CELSIUS(C) (APPROXIMATE)
225 °F	107 °C
250 °F	120 °C
275 °F	135 °C
300 °F	150 °C
325 °F	160 °C
350 °F	180 °C
375 °F	190 °C
400 °F	205 °C
425 °F	220 °C
450 °F	235 °C
475 °F	245 °C
500 °F	260 °C

APPENDIX RECIPES INDEX

Made in the USA
Las Vegas, NV
28 December 2024